The Power of Mobile Banking

The Power of Mobile Banking

How to Profit from the Revolution in Retail Financial Services

SANKAR KRISHNAN

WILEY

Library of Congress Cataloging-in-Publication Data:

ISBN 978-1-118-91424-3 (Hardcover)
ISBN 978-1-118-93203-2 (ePDF)
ISBN 978-1-118-93204-9 (ePub)

Printed in the United States of America
10 9 8 7 6 5 4 3 2 1

To my family and friends

Contents

Foreword

Mobile banking is upon us. The rise of the mobile device combined with the increased value of mobile business has made mobile the most important channel for the future of banking. And because mobile devices allow for significant innovation, they will quickly transform retail banking across the world.

Forecasts estimate that more than one billion people will be using mobile banking by 2017. But the number might be even larger than that. Consumers want a personal customer experience from their banks, and mobile delivers a personal, tailored experience better than any other technology.

And while many cite security as a concern for not using mobile banking, that excuse is not grounded in truth. The truth is that mobile banking is as secure, and maybe more secure, than online banking. Complaining about security is simply a weak excuse for those who will be left behind.

So why aren't market leaders driving the mobile channel? After all, established banks and investment firms are in the best position to capitalize on the positive changes coming from mobile banking. They have the ability to make the biggest difference because they have the required resources and capital to invest in mobile innovations.

Yet those same established companies are often the most reluctant to embrace the changes. They own market share, but just owning market share does not guarantee success. Future success will go to the agile and adaptive companies;

those companies that recognize and develop the new mobile opportunities.

Recognition and development of the mobile channel is hard for some companies because it is not just a technological phenomenon; it is also a psychological and sociological phenomenon. Mobile innovation requires the recognition of change and the ability to embrace it. Banks will have to change their operational expertise to encompass mobile banking and adapt their processes and products to meet the new needs. They need a model and a strategy that positions mobile as a main priority instead of an afterthought.

It's not about technology, it's about change. They will have to become ambidextrous—able to run their current transactional business on one hand while developing and innovating their mobile innovations on the other hand. This is no small task as most large banks are still led by transactional leaders. The difference between a transactional leader and a transformational leader is impactful.

Transactional leaders tend to passively work within the current systems and only change when they absolutely must, while transformational leaders are willing to immediately change the way things are done. And even though we can see that bold, mobile strategies will win the day, so many large banks are still satisfied with the status quo and current transactions.

Contrary to traditional banks, startups understand the importance of mobile and are using it to gain market share. And nontraditional competitors like Internet and telecommunications companies are positioning themselves to exploit the mobile banking market. Meanwhile traditional banks and market leaders are watching it all happen. That's why this book is needed.

Sankar's perspective is essential and well-timed for anyone in the banking business, but is especially valuable for the established banks who currently own significant market share. Established banks truly need a wake-up call from a trusted expert within the industry, and Sankar is the right person. As a long-time banking practitioner and innovator, he provides real world expertise versus theories and concepts. He skillfully wraps the thoughts and wisdom of other leading practitioners into the storyline so that we all benefit.

And from the lens of an Indian-born citizen who understands international banking, Sankar brings the valuable viewpoint of one of the largest growing economies in the world, and a primary market from which reverse innovation is occurring. Most of all, Sankar's desire to help others comes through in this valuable book.

There is no industry in a better position to help others than the world's leading banks, and there is no greater channel for that help than mobile. That's why this book is a must-read for financial services practitioners and a must-heed for their leaders.

—Mick Simonelli

Preface

When I began writing this book, I quickly realized that I was stuck between a rock and a hard place. I wanted the book to be thoroughly and carefully researched. As a corporate business executive, I believe firmly in the value of research and I do not take it lightly. That said, I also knew that I was racing against the clock. In addition to the publisher's deadline, the world around me was changing fast. I knew on a gut level that the longer it took me to write the manuscript, the more outdated the book would be when it was eventually published.

So I tried to split the difference. I crammed as much research as I possibly could into a brief span of about six months, and converted my research into decent prose as expeditiously as possible. The result is a mixed bag. If you are new to the themes and topics covered in the book, you will find them fresh and exciting. If you are a career banker or investor, you might find yourself thinking, "I already know a lot of this." If those thoughts enter your mind, I urge you to keep reading. I have tried to include a wide variety of interesting material, harvested from a broad range of sources. Even if you are the most experienced banker in the world, you will likely find new and valuable information on these pages.

Here is a brief road map of what to expect in this book: In Chapter 1, we look at the power and potential of mobile banking. As a strategy, mobile banking is not a one-size-fits-all solution. In developed markets, mobile banking offers banks a great opportunity for reducing costs, delivering better service, and reaching a new generation of consumers. In emerging or underdeveloped markets, mobile is a major driver of economic growth. In many parts of India, China, Africa, the Middle East, and Latin America, mobile devices now deliver services that in the past required huge investments in physical infrastructure. In many instances, mobile lets a country skip over the infrastructure challenge and move directly to providing the essential services required by a rising consumer class.

In Chapter 2, we review the current state of retail banking and discuss the historical trends that have led us to this point. Banking has a rich history and has evolved continuously over time to meet the needs of new markets and new groups of customers. Mobile banking is the most recent example of how savvy bankers have adopted new technologies and put them to work to deliver more services, grow their businesses, and make greater profits.

In Chapter 3, we look at the impact of "Generation M," also known as the millennial generation or the mobile generation. We talk about how, as a culture, our habits of consumption have changed. The old paradigm of "touch and smell" has been replaced by a new paradigm of "see and hear." As bankers, we need to get over our collective shock and accept the fact that the world around us has changed. We need to make sure that our products and services remain relevant and essential to a new generation of digital natives and tech-savvy consumers.

Chapter 4 examines the expanding role of mobile payment systems and reveals how such systems offer a new universe of opportunities for banks that are willing to make the right investments in the people, processes, and technologies required to implement and support mobile platforms. Mobile banking also creates opportunities for banks to offer consumer-friendly informational services to their customers via their mobile devices. Mobile will also accelerate the continuing growth of e-commerce, which opens up many new and potentially profitable ways for banks to engage consumers. Banks should aim for channel efficiency, which means offering the best possible customer experiences at the lowest possible costs.

Chapter 5 is a detailed examination of the practical aspects of mobile banking. I also offer some tips and advice that many consultants neglect to mention. I caution mobile bankers to look before they leap and to be fully prepared. Plan out exactly what you want to achieve with your mobile strategy, and make sure that everyone understands what you're doing. Get the right players and start building teams to execute your strategy. In addition to application (app) developers, you will need information technology (IT) suppliers, integrators, and consultants to make sure that all the technology works together smoothly and seamlessly. Don't forget about costs and pricing. Typically, mobile is seen as a low-cost channel. But customers should also see it as a preferred channel. Make sure that it delivers truly excellent service and benefits to users, and that it offers real value and unique features.

In Chapter 6, we delve into the world of prepaid cards. Few bankers consider the prepaid card market to be sexy, but it has its uses. So my advice to bankers is simple: Don't ignore the potential of prepaid cards. While they might not be the ideal solution, they are widely used and accepted. Worldwide, prepaid cards represent a great opportunity for growth and market penetration. The prepaid card market is experiencing double-digit year-over-year growth in multiple markets in numerous countries, including the United States, Brazil, Mexico, Italy, India, Canada, Russia, and parts of the Middle East. Worldwide, total loadable volume is expected to reach nearly $1 trillion.

Chapter 7 is a no-holds-barred discussion of the risks and hazards of mobile banking. There's no point in sugarcoating the problems and headaches you will encounter, so you might as well be ready for them. Most bankers think of mobile banking risks in terms of device security. But the real issue is the potential loss of customers and market share. As nonbank entities enter the mobile banking market, loss of market share is a fundamental and strategic risk. Banks must be willing and able to make critical investments in mobile technologies, or they risk losing their customers to nonbank players such as telecoms, retailers, and technology providers.

Chapter 8 looks at the bigger picture, revealing areas in which mobile technology is sure to become an important, and possibly even dominant, force. Mobile banking opens the door to a variety of potentially important mobile services such as mobile health care, mobile education, mobile marketing, mobile manufacturing, and many other new ways of interacting with customers. Mobile banking represents a subset of the emerging mobile economy, which has the potential to bring greater wealth and happiness to billions of people all over the world.

Indeed, the world is changing at an inconceivably fast pace. What seemed fresh and new yesterday seems old hat today. That's the strange nature of modernity, and it explains why millions of people find the modern world a frightening place. I'm always a little disappointed when leaders who ought to know better try to guide us backward instead of forward. For me, the past is a treasure trove of knowledge and tradition. But I am also keenly aware that the past can serve only as a template or a rough guide. We live in the present and we are responsible for inventing our own futures. That is why we constantly strive to learn and to understand what is happening in the world around us. When we understand something, we no longer fear it. We move ahead boldly, we improve our lives and the lives of our families, and we achieve the satisfaction of knowing that we did our best.

I hope that this book will help you learn more about a fascinating and truly vibrant part of our global economy, and that it will contribute in some small way to your success and happiness.

Acknowledgments

Much of this book is based on my own experiences as a bank executive. Naturally, it reflects my own opinions and thoughts about the banking industry.

This book is also a work of journalism, however, and I have relied on the testimonies of many expert sources to tell the stories contained in these pages. For their time, energy, advice, and insight, I am indebted to Scott Bales, Rameshwar N. Bhargava, Steve Blank, Annetta Cortez, Michael Faye, Greg Fell, Ajay Hans, Matthew Holt, Farhad Irani, Neal Kaufman, Brett King, Harvey Koeppel, Art Mannarn, Jim Marous, Phillip M. Miller, Stan Nowak, Todd Nuttall, Don Peppers, Banesh Prabhu, Narayanan Ram, Carlo Ratti, Greg Satell, Mick Simonelli, Chris Skinner, Steven J. Smith, Danny Tang, Jonathan Teich, Jim Tosone, and Edward van Eckert.

I also wish to thank my editors at John Wiley & Sons, including Sheck Cho, Stacey Rivera, and Chris Gage. I owe a special debt of gratitude to Mike Barlow, who served as editorial director and producer of this project. Without Mike's support and persistence, this book would not have been possible. Thanks, Mike!

CHAPTER 1

The Power and Potential of Mobile Banking

Why I Wrote This Book

Growing up in Madras, India, in the 1980s, I saw firsthand the impact of the digital revolution on one of the world's largest and most populous nations. Overnight, it seemed, India's middle class grew by every measure.

To me, the power of mobile communications to change the lives of people and radically transform an economy isn't something imaginary or theoretical. It's very real. I saw it happen, with my own eyes.

I realize that mobile was just one of many inputs driving the rise of the middle class in India.[1] But in my childhood memories, mobile technology and money are inextricably linked.

In developing markets, mobile is a major driver of economic growth. In many parts of India, China, Africa, the Middle East, and Latin America, mobile devices now deliver services that in the past required huge investments in physical infrastructure. In many instances, mobile lets a country skip over the infrastructure challenge, and move directly to providing the essential services required by a rising consumer class.

I have also seen what failed economies look like, and frankly, they aren't a pretty sight. As a young Citibank executive, I had the opportunity to cover several of the emerging economies, including some of the post-war development effort (from a financial sector perspective) in Afghanistan. Through implementing financial structures together with the World Bank and the United Nations, banks like Citi (and their peers with a focus on developing economies) were able to ensure that goods and services reached the people who needed them. I remember thinking that if more people in places such as Afghanistan, Iraq and Bosnia had mobile phones, we could have easily created a system for monitoring the progress of the trucks carrying the supplies we dispatched, ensuring that the supplies reached their proper destinations and keeping track of how they were used by the people who actually received them.

A system like that wouldn't have required lots of infrastructure. A decent mobile network and a handful of mobile phones would have made a big difference in the lives of those poor people.

I'm a banker. I'm not trying to save the world. But I do believe that mobile is part of the solution to many problems, in both developed economies and undeveloped economies. Mobile can also become a huge driver of profit, for businesses large and small, all over the world.

Most important, mobile has the power to change radically the way we live and how we interact with each other and, more increasingly, with the machines and automated systems that serve our needs.

Today, we apply the term *mobile devices* mostly to phones and tablets. Tomorrow, the term will include clothing, watches, jewelry, medicine, household appliances, cars, trucks, boats, airplanes—everything we make or use will be connected to a mobile network.

What my friends at General Electric call the "Industrial Internet" and Cisco calls "The Internet of Things" or the "Internet of Everything" is growing every day, and mobile is one of the prime forces driving its development.

Think Behavior, Not Technology

For banks and bankers, a caveat: Mobile is not a free pass; it's more like a Chance card from the board game Monopoly that moves you quickly across the board. Sometimes you pass Go and collect $200, but sometimes you don't.

The easiest way to fumble the mobile opportunity will be to see mobile banking as a technological phenomenon. That would be an error of epic proportions. Mobile banking is a global behavioral phenomenon, or more accurately, it is the result of significant behavioral changes that have been occurring all over the world since the introduction of the Internet and the World Wide Web.

The shift to mobile banking isn't being driven by technology; it's being driven by psychology. People today just don't see the world the same way that people did 30 years ago. Millennials understand the new reality because that's all they know. Those of us who grew up as baby boomers or Gen Xers will just have to do our best to understand what's going on, and get with the new program before it's too late.

Please take a moment to consider some of the U.S. Federal Reserve data in the charts below. The charts show survey data on the use of mobile banking technology as of March 2012. As you can see from the data, the use of mobile banking correlates with age, income, and education.

USE OF MOBILE BANKING IS CORRELATED BY AGE OF USER (%)

Age Categories	YES	NO	Total
18–29	43.5	16.8	22.4
30–44	35.7	24.7	27.0
45–59	14.7	30.2	26.9
60 Plus	6.1	28.4	23.7
Number of Respondents	372	1,626	1,998

Source: U.S. Federal Reserve

USE OF MOBILE BANKING BY INCOME GROUP (%)

Income Group	Yes	No	Total
< $25,000	12.8	19.9	18.4
$25,000–$39,999	19.0	16.6	17.1
$40,000–$74,999	27.5	26.5	26.7
$75,000–$99,999	12.9	14.0	13.8
$100,000 or greater	27.9	22.9	24.0
Number of Respondents	372	1,626	1,998

Source: U.S. Federal Reserve

USE OF MOBILE BANKING BY EDUCATION GROUP (%)

Education	Yes	No	Total
Less than High School	5.5	12.1	10.7
High School	21.5	31.8	29.6
Some College	39.0	27.4	29.8
Bachelor's degree or higher	34.0	28.8	29.9
Number of Respondents	372	1,626	1,998

Source: U.S. Federal Reserve

"We're at a crossroads now," says my friend Scott Bales, a founding member of Moven and the innovation director at Next Bank. "Mobile is changing our ideas of how the world works. In the past, when you needed information, you went to a library. When you needed a book, you went to a bookstore. When you needed your favorite recording artist's newest album, you went to a record store. Today, you can do all of that on your mobile device—you don't have to *go* somewhere to *do* something."

The idea that *doing something* no longer requires *going somewhere* represents a huge transformation in human behavior. That behavioral transformation is the driving force behind mobile banking.

"Most banks don't understand what's happening. They think it's all about technology, when really it's all about behaviors," says Scott. Banks that don't want to join the party blame perceived inadequacies in technology for sticking with the status quo. "They are desperately clinging to the past. Rather than act on the many opportunities offered by mobile banking, they prefer spreading fear, uncertainty, and doubt," says Scott. "They will talk about security issues, even though mobile technology is far more secure than any of the incumbent technologies."

Some of Moven's mobile banking interfaces are shown below:

Essentially, he says, many traditional banks would prefer to ignore mobile banking. But that won't be easy. "First, the customer base is changing as more millennials enter the workforce and begin climbing up through the corporate ranks. Second, those millennials are going to start making critical business decisions at the companies they work for. Why would they partner

FIGURE 1.1 Categories

Source: Moven. Used with permission.

5

FIGURE 1.2 Home Screen

Source: Moven. Used with permission.

with banks that don't have mobile strategies?" Scott makes a terrific point here. Banks that don't get their mobile acts together will be putting more than just their individual consumer retail accounts at risk—they will also risk losing their larger and very profitable corporate accounts!

As if that weren't enough of an incentive to get with the program, Scott raises another key potential risk: losing the confidence of investors. "It's only a matter of time before we see the investment community downgrading the valuations of banks that don't have their digital acts together," says Scott.

I agree wholeheartedly with him. When I see a bank that doesn't offer a full range of digital services, including mobile banking, I start wondering what's wrong with its information technology (IT) organization. For me, and for other professionals

FIGURE 1.3 Receipts

Source: Moven. Used with permission.

in the business, mobile services are becoming a proxy for technical competency. If you're a bank in a hypercompetitive market, do you really want to send the world a clear signal that you're behind the technology curve?

"Mobile banking is more important as a behavior than as a technology," says Scott. "As a culture, our behavioral norms have changed. Facebook, Twitter, Netflix, Spotify, and Google have fundamentally transformed the way people interact with the world around them. It's not just banking that will have to change—every business and every industry will feel the impact. They will either adapt or die."

To my mind, Scott has really picked up on the zeitgeist and understands the big picture. He's in the flow, and he seems to have an intuitive sense of where all of this is heading.

7

That said, I'll end this section with a great quote from the legendary innovator and venture capitalist Marc Andreessen:

Today, ask kids if they'd rather have a smartphone or a car if they had to pick and 100% would say smartphones. Because smartphones represent freedom. There's a huge social behavior reorientation that's already happening.[2]

Why Mobile Banking, and Why Now?

From an internal perspective, I find it helpful to think of mobile banking as both a creative functional solution and a viable business platform. Mobile banking is like an automated teller machine (ATM) on steroids—it's a highly functional *and* highly cost-effective alternative to a branch office. Mobile technology enables a bank to interact with a customer in a variety of ways that are both practical and potentially profitable for both parties—without the costs normally associated with operating a branch office.

From an external perspective, it's more helpful to see mobile banking as a product or a service designed to make banking more convenient for customers. Customers need convenience, safety, access, low transaction costs, speed, continuity, and a sense of security. Mobile banking delivers on all of those needs.

Mobile banking is more than the newest bright, shiny object. It is not the flavor of the month; it is not a fad. It represents a clear break with the past—a past that required customers to stop whatever they were doing and "go somewhere" whenever they needed a banking service.

Mobile banking takes the location requirement out of banking. This is a critical concept, this notion that mobile technology renders your location largely irrelevant. With mobile banking, you never have to find a branch. All you have to do is find your phone!

Fortunately, there appears to be no shortage of mobile phones or tablets. At the beginning of 2013, there were 6.8 billion mobile subscriptions worldwide, compared to 6 billion the previous year and 5.4 billion the year before that.[3] Portio Research estimates that by the end of 2016 there will be 8.5 billion mobile subscribers worldwide.[4] Portio notes that markets in the Asia-Pacific region and Africa will lead the surge in mobile users.

Here's an interesting excerpt from "Africa's Information Revolution: Implications for Crime, Policing, and Citizen Security," a fascinating research paper from the Africa Center for Strategic Studies, written by Steven Livingston:

> *Africa has seen a 20 percent increase in mobile phone subscriptions for each of the past 5 years, growing from 2 percent of the population in 2000 to 63 percent by the end of 2012. In early 2013, Africa had the second fastest mobile telephony growth rate (after China) in the world with 775 million cellular connections across the continent. In South Africa, Ghana, Gabon, and Kenya, there are already nearly as many mobile accounts as there are people. By 2015, Sub-Saharan Africa may have more people with mobile network access than with access to electricity at home. These individuals will increasingly be able to make video calls, watch video clips, or access the Internet on their mobile phones. While much of the growth in mobile telephony in Africa involves simple first- and second-generation handsets, more recent growth includes Internet-enabled smartphones. By 2018, 40–50 percent of all mobiles in Africa may have access to the Internet.[5]*

The United States, of course, isn't immune to the effects of the mobile phenomenon. Depending on which surveys you look at, it seems clear that around one-third of U.S. households have already dropped their wired landlines and opted for mobile. A USTelecom filing with the Federal Communications Commission

(FCC) in late 2012, for example, estimates that 44 percent of U.S. households will have unwired by the end of 2013.[6]

Take a quick look at what research site mobiThinking says about the onslaught of mobile:

> *Mobile subscriptions outnumber fixed lines 6:1 (more so in developing nations); Mobile broadband outnumbers fixed broadband 3:1. With stats like this, it is easy to see why the experts predict that mobile Web usage will overtake PC-based Web usage. This will happen more quickly in developing nations—in China and other countries it already has—where fixed Web penetration remains low. In developed nations, this will happen more slowly. IDC [International Data Corporation] believes that mobile Web usage will not overtake PC Web usage in the US until 2015. Regardless of the timescale, this inevitability makes your mobile Web strategy more important than your PC Web strategy in the long term.[7]*

I include the extended quote because it's a good segue to an important point: Do not confuse your online strategy with your mobile strategy. They are not the same thing; they are very different, and they require radically different approaches. Unquestionably, online banking is a great tool and a major convenience for bank customers in the developed world. But online banking requires a personal computer (PC) or a tablet with a web browser. The advantage of mobile banking is that all the customer needs is a mobile phone and your mobile banking application (app).

Sanity Checks

I live in the United States, and I travel a great deal. That said, my perspective on the world is mostly limited to information I glean from books, reports, and white papers; from my personal

10

experiences, such as conversations with other bankers; from browsing the web; and from attending a wide variety of professional seminars, summits, and colloquiums.

During the process of writing this book, I reached out frequently to peers and colleagues in other parts of the world and asked them what they think about this whole mobile banking phenomenon. Talking (or e-mailing or texting) with old friends is often a pleasant way to pass the time while traveling. There is also a practical side to my sociability: My friends serve as sounding boards, and more important, as sanity checks, for the ideas and notions that occur to me as I write.

One of the friends I contacted early in the writing process was Farhad Irani, the executive vice president and group head of retail banking at Mashreq Bank, the United Arab Emirates' largest and fastest-growing privately owned financial institution. Mashreq has operations in 12 countries, and has received many awards for quality and innovation.

Farhad has three decades of work experience in payments, retail banking, and e-commerce space. He has served in executive posts at PayPal, Standard Chartered Bank, Citibank Japan, and Korea Exchange Bank, and has lived in India, Indonesia, South Korea, Japan, Singapore, Hong Kong, and Dubai. I mention all of that because it demonstrates the depth and range of his experience and knowledge of the banking industry.

He sees mobile technology as driving "the biggest economic revolution we will see in our lifetimes. In the developed world, it will give financial institutions the ability to reengineer their end-to-end processes. It will create many new conveniences for consumers." In the developing world, mobile will translate into "financial inclusion" that reduces poverty, creates new wealth, and empowers billions of people to raise their standard of living.

11

He does not see mobile as a threat to existing financial institutions, since "mobile customers will tend to consolidate their main bank relationship" with one institution offering the services they use most often. To me, that's a clear signal that banks must offer a full suite of robust mobile services if they want to retain their existing customers and acquire new, younger customers.

"Mobile is increasingly becoming more secure than Internet banking, and there have been huge innovations on the back end of mobile technology, enabling a wider range of payments," says Farhad. "Payments are the most important part of the retail banking spectrum. If you lose payments, you lose the customer."

For ordinary consumers, Farhad sees mobile banking as a true bonanza. "It brings convenience to the consumer. It's more secure and more confidential, and it will allow consumers to switch banks more easily."

On the business side, Farhad predicts that mobile will enable banks to greatly improve their customer relationship management processes, provide much more relevant marketing through real-time alerts based on geospatial information, leverage big data to speed up loan approvals and extend credit, and do an all-around better job of serving customers wherever they are.

He also foresees better relationships with customers through face-to-face video interactions with customer service representatives, delivered via existing mobile technologies. In other words, a customer's experience with the bank's call center will become less of a faceless interaction between two disembodied voices and more of a personal dialogue between two human beings, thanks to mobile video.

"We're living in exciting and dynamic times," says Farhad. "Mobile allows a huge opportunity to transform the banking experience and create higher levels of engagement in the realm of personal financial services. Mobile is the future. Tablet sales in the last three years have outstripped the sales of PCs. Cost of network and strength of network double every 18 months, cost of hardware halves every 18 months, and over one billion smartphones will be delivered in 2014. For people and institutions that can accept change, this will be a great period of growth and development."

I wholeheartedly agree. In his characteristically diplomatic fashion, Farhad implies an *if* in his prediction of great times ahead. Mobile can be enormously transformational, but only *if* we are willing to accept the changes it will inevitably bring.

Looking at the Opportunities and Challenges

I asked my friend Art Mannarn for his list of the greatest opportunities and challenges associated with mobile banking. Art is Executive Vice President and Chief Administrative Officer, Retail & Business Banking at Canadian Imperial Bank of Commerce (CIBC), which gives him a great view into the current state of banking. From Art's perspective, the opportunities include:

- Redefining the client experience to more fully leverage digital processes, work flows, and information to enable a more robust experience
- Driving costs out of the system through improved self-service options, lower defect rates on applications, and straight-through processing
- Creating additional touch points to enable more customized interactions with clients on terms that they prefer
- Enabling a higher level of convenience for clients: banking at any time, through any channel

"Retail banking leaders are specifically investing in the redesign and integration of digital capabilities to enable the delivery of seamless, highly convenient mobile banking platforms for clients," says Art.

The key challenges he sees retail banks facing include:

- The investment required, including the need to have leading experts helping to shape and execute on a mobile strategy
- Achieving tight integration and synchronization across multiple client touch points
- Keeping ahead of the rapid pace of innovation in mobile banking: new technologies, new smartphones, new entrants, and so forth

I also asked him how, from an organizational perspective, banks should prepare for a world in which mobile devices are increasingly the go-to choice for consumers. Here are Art's suggestions:

- Be less reliant on processes and standards that were built to principally serve the off-line experience.
- Ensure that the people driving the strategy and implementation understand the digital reality.
- Create opportunities to enable integration across the disparate communities of interest and skill within the organization.
- Remain current with the capabilities and issues associated with the increasingly wide range of mobile devices, technologies, and manufacturers.

It is truly impressive how Art breaks the issue down into its component parts. That's the hallmark of a true visionary, in my opinion! That said, I also asked Art for his perspective on how mobile banking will change the way that consumers relate to banks. Here are his thoughts:

- Clients expect the bank to be responsive, in real time, to their requests delivered through any channel at virtually any time of the day.
- Their expectations around speed of service also extend to high expectations around the bank's knowledge of them, their specific needs, and their overall relationship with the bank.
- Clients no longer have the same need for face-to-face interactions, so the quality of online interactions needs to improve to enable advice delivery as well as service.
- Banks that cross the digital divide will remain relevant; those that do not will gradually lose their relevance to today's consumers.

Finally, I asked Art to list specific benefits and advantages that mobile technology brings to banks and their clients. Here are his responses:

- Mobile technology enables banks to deliver highly relevant and tailored interactions to their clients, driving improved client engagement and reduced operating costs.
- It enables much more precise targeting of clients, at a fraction of conventional marketing outreach techniques.
- It delivers a much richer experience to clients in terms of self-directed advice, service, and research.
- It provides opportunities for real-time decision making and customization of products and services.

"The financial services industry is placing a greater focus on providing mobile banking solutions for clients, and those who execute better in this area will have the opportunity to competitively differentiate from the rest," says Art.

Time to Rock the Boat

In a hypercompetitive world, in which every new product or service quickly becomes a commodity, you either innovate or die. Innovation is no longer a luxury; it's a basic requirement for staying in business and competing successfully.

For a variety of reasons, some more legitimate than others, the banking industry has been slow to embrace innovation. The traditional reluctance of banks to rock the boat is understandable—we are, after all, a heavily regulated industry. And we have a long, long history. Banks have been around for roughly 4,000 years. That makes us one of the oldest continuously operating industries in the world!

The banking industry has certainly accomplished a lot over the past four millennia. It's hard to imagine how any modern economy—or any modern civilization—could exist without a robust banking system. In addition to our many accomplishments, however, we have built up a large store of inertia. If we want to remain competitive and relevant as an industry, we need to overcome some of that inertia and begin moving more swiftly into newer markets and serving newer populations of customers.

Who are those new customers, and where do they live? In the United States, most of Europe, and parts of the Middle East, they are the millennials, the generation of digital natives who will soon inherit the world's developed economies.

In the rest of the world, those new customers include everyone who doesn't currently have a bank account. Please read this brief excerpt from the Bill & Melinda Gates Foundation website:

Worldwide, approximately 2.5 billion people do not have a formal account at a financial institution, according to the World Bank's Global Financial Inclusion Database. As a result, most poor households operate almost entirely in the cash economy, particularly in the developing world.[8]

That's a staggering number of people—and from my perspective, it represents enormous potential for banks that are willing to look beyond their existing base of customers in the developed world.

Make no mistake—the unbanked and underbanked are fertile soil for business growth. In developed nations, those potential customers tend to be young. In underdeveloped or developing nations, they tend to be poor or living in rural areas. But here's what they have in common: They use mobile phones.

Mobile phones and mobile technologies are the keys for reaching those unserved or underserved populations, and converting them into profitable banking customers. In many situations, mobile will be one of several channels deployed in a broader strategy of customer acquisition and growth. In some situations, mobile will be the preeminent or primary channel for business growth.

In some situations, mobile banking will require the development of new systems of payment, and in some instances, the development of new kinds of money. It won't be easy, but it won't be insurmountably difficult.

The main attraction of mobile banking is that practically all the necessary infrastructure already exists. You don't have to build anything from the ground up—all you have to do is figure out how to apply the existing mobile infrastructure to banking!

From the perspective of many of us in the banking industry, the partnership of banks and mobile network operators (MNOs) seems like a winning combination: Banks gain access to untapped markets, and MNOs retain more customers (the thought being that customers are less likely to defect if their bank accounts are somehow tied to their mobile subscriptions).

17

Indisputably, the full picture is complex, "involving many players (e.g., banks, mobile-money operators, processors), channels for accessing cash or making transactions (e.g., ATMs, point-of-sale terminals, online interfaces, mobile phones), and payment instruments that can be used to make transactions (e.g., credit transfers, debit cards, credit cards)."[9]

But imagine the payoff. We've looked briefly at the potential size of the market for mobile banking. Now let's consider the economic dimensions. The U.S. General Accountability Office (GAO) estimates that as many as 56 million adults—roughly one-fifth of all adults in the United States—are unbanked or underbanked. As a group, they "spend $10.9 billion on more than 324 million alternative financial transactions, including check cashing and payday loans, every year," according to a recent Diebold white paper.[10]

Extrapolating from those figures suggests an untapped global market of about $500 billion. I wouldn't bet the farm on that estimate, but it certainly raises a compelling question: Why would the banking industry leave that kind of money lying on the table?

Here's my fear: If we, as an industry, don't address the financial needs of the millennials, the unbanked, and the under-banked, another industry certainly will. In some nations, retail stores offer banklike services to customers.

Worldwide, companies such as eBay, Amazon, and Apple operate like virtual banks. Every day, it seems, another start-up unveils a new mobile payment app. It feels like the early days of the California Gold Rush. Nobody knows exactly where the gold is, but they know it's out there somewhere. And they are rushing past us to make sure that they stake a claim before someone else does.

Are we going to stand idly by and let a bunch of newcomers eat our lunch? I hope not. I believe that the means of salvation are at hand. For years, we have focused on cultivating our

18

best and wealthiest customers. We have spent countless hours and innumerable dollars trying to determine the best locations for new bank branches, and we have invested hundreds of millions of dollars to build, acquire, or rent the space where the branches are located.

Every year, we spend hundreds of millions to staff and maintain the branches, and every year, we close or relocate thousands of branches. Maybe we should be in the commercial real estate business instead of the banking business!

Focusing on the Customer Experience

There's a healthier alternative. Mobile banking frees us from worrying about the need to build and staff physical branches, and empowers us to focus exclusively on the customer experience, which takes place entirely on the customer's mobile device.

In many parts of the developing world, the lack of roads and infrastructure makes it virtually impossible to construct a network of physical branches. In the developing world, mobile banking is clearly the smartest and most practical way for a bank to build its brand.

Focusing on nonwealthy customers isn't a pipe dream, and I certainly didn't invent the idea. In a seminal white paper published by *Strategy + Business* in 2002, C. K. Prahalad and Stuart Hart lay out the principles for a business vision that's sharply focused on the four billion people at the bottom of the world's wealth pyramid—the zone described by the authors as the "BoP." In the paper,[11] which is a truly amazing work of insight and creativity, Prahalad and Hart make a stunning yet totally logical assertion: Depending on your perspective, those four billion people at the bottom of the pyramid represent either an intractable problem or an excellent opportunity for a new generation of smart businesses.

19

As you can imagine, I prefer the latter perspective. Prahalad and Hart estimate that the potential purchasing power of the BoP market is more than $13 trillion. At the risk of repeating myself, the BoP market is simply too big a market to overlook or dismiss.

In their excellent book, *Abundance: The Future Is Better Than You Think*, Peter H. Diamandis and Steven Kotler offer a great summary of the BoP concept. I recommend the book highly, and it is especially relevant to the banking industry. The authors write:

> *M-banking allows people to check their balances, pay bills, receive payments, and send money home without giant transfer fees, as well as avoid the increased personal security risks that come from carrying cash.*
>
> *. . . [M]obile banking has seen exponential growth in a few short years. M-PESA, launched in Kenya in 2007 by Safaricom, had 20,000 customers its first month. Four months later, it had 150,000; four years after than, 13 million.*[12]

Diamandis and Hart underscore the idea that immense opportunities await those willing to accept the challenges of the emerging BoP market. Far from being an ordinary market, it is a "radically different business environment" requiring "radically different business strategies," write the authors. Mobile, by nature, is perfectly suited for developing, enabling, and supporting those radical business strategies.

New Models for Charity

Although I am first and foremost a banker, I certainly don't want to give you the impression that all I care about is making money. I am deeply concerned about the unequal distribution of wealth across our beautiful planet, and I also believe strongly that when people have access to money, the world becomes a better place. Wealth begets wealth, and oftentimes you have to prime the pump to get a local economy going.

That's why I read with interest about GiveDirectly, an organization that channels donations directly—and without strings attached—to poor people in Kenya and Uganda, via their mobile phones. We spoke recently with GiveDirectly's cofounder and chairman of the board, Michael Faye. He explained to us how the organization's approach differs from the standard charity model.

"The World Economic Forum estimates that $400 billion is transferred annually from emerging market governments to individuals as cash transfers. A substantial portion of that money is transferred in antiquated ways and there is a lot of leakage. One of our goals is serving that market and reducing the leakage to as close to zero as possible," says Michael.

GiveDirectly's broader goal, however, is fundamentally altering the ways in which donated cash is distributed to poor people. "The question we're asking is, would the poor do more good with the money than the charities? In a lot of cases, the answer would be yes," he says.

The organization has created a model that looks something like an index fund with clear performance benchmarks. In other words, GiveDirectly doesn't just throw cash at poor people. Instead, it uses modern technology and corporate-style business accounting practices to make sure the money reaches its intended destination, efficiently and transparently.

"Not everyone in a village in western Kenya needs the same thing. Some need money to send their kids to school. Others need money to start a small business. Some just need money to rebuild their roofs," he explains. "The problem with many charities is that they assume there's a one-size-fits-all model."

For example, a charity might decide to send a cow to each village in a certain area. But not every village needs a cow. "So they sell it for cash to buy the things they *do* need," says Michael.

GiveDirectly's approach is inexpensive, scalable, auditable, and transparent. "We can literally track where every dollar goes and the impact it's having," he says.

Here's a quick overview of how the process works: First, the organization picks a location based on its level of poverty. Then a team is dispatched to the location (usually a village) and a highly detailed map is created, using modern digital data collection techniques. "The team literally goes house to house and gathers data, everything from GPS coordinates to the materials used to construct the house," says Michael. Then a second team is sent in to register people in the village and verify the data collected by the first team. Having two data sets enables the organization to operate with a high level of certainty. "We compare the data sets and make sure they're valid. If someone says they live in a certain house, we can verify that with GPS data and by the type of material used to build the house," he says.

Only after another team has been dispatched to the village to triple-check the data will the organization authorize token payments to make sure the money gets to where it's supposed to go. If no problems or issues arise, more payments are authorized. In Kenya, villagers receive direct payments through their M-Pesa accounts. In Uganda, they receive payments through other mobile-based systems.

As Michael says, it's an approach that can be easily scaled and audited. I think it's the future of charity in the developing world. "Charity has become a dirty word. We see ourselves as service providers," says Michael.

Transparent processes and redundancy are the keys to the organization's success. "We require our staff to go door to door to register people," explains Michael. In one instance, Michael says that he could see from the GPS data that agents had assembled villagers in a field or schoolyard to register them instead of going door to door. The agents were dismissed.

Indeed, GiveDirectly takes its data seriously. "We send three and sometimes four teams to collect the same data, and then we match it," says Michael. In keeping with its commitment to evaluate the impact of its programs accurately, GiveDirectly is conducting a randomized controlled trial—an activity that is virtually unheard of in the charity sector. The trial results have shown increases in income, decreases in hunger, reduction of stress levels, and reduced conflict, says Michael.

From my own experiences in the field, I know the importance of accuracy, consistency, and thoroughness. GiveDirectly is more than a pioneer; it is a role model for all of us who are interested in making a better world.

Is That a Bank in Your Pocket, or Are You Just Happy to See Me?

There are also plenty of good reasons to question the value of physical branches in developed economies. When was the last time you saw a millennial standing in line at a bank branch? I think it's fair to say that millennials have little affinity for bank branches.

If given a choice between making a transaction on a mobile device and visiting a bank branch, I feel confident that the typical millennial would choose the former and not the latter. For digital natives, using a mobile device feels a lot more comfortable and convenient than making a trip to the bank. You don't even have to change out of your pajamas!

If you're part of the baby boom or Generation Y, there's a chance that you might feel sentimental about your local bank branch. But I guarantee you that millennials experience no similar sense of nostalgia. For them, bank branches are for people who can't figure out how to use a mobile banking app.

You might be thinking, "Well, who cares? Those kids don't have big accounts and certainly they aren't our most profitable customers." Just remember this: Today they might not be valuable customers. But tomorrow, when they have jobs and mortgages and stock portfolios, they probably will be valuable customers. Are you willing to cede them, along with their lifetime value as customers, to your competitors?

You can make a similar case for paying more attention to unbanked and underbanked people in the developing world. It would be easy to ignore them, but that would be a grave mistake. Nobody expected the middle class to rise as quickly as it did in China. It seems like it happened overnight, or during the blink of an eye. Are you so sure that similar miracles won't occur in South Asia, Africa, and Latin America?

Remember, there are 2.5 billion people out there without bank accounts, and not all of them are desperately poor. Many are just looking for a safe place to keep their money and conduct their financial transactions. Sounds to me like they are looking for a good bank.

Evolution or Revolution?

Chris Skinner is author of a new book, *Digital Bank*,[13] chair of a bank network in Europe called the Financial Services Club, and a regular commentator on BBC News, Sky News, and Bloomberg about banking issues.

From his point of view, there are two prevailing theories on how banks will get "from here to there" in terms of mobile banking strategy. The first theory holds that banks will evolve, much as they have in the past, gradually adapting to the changing world around them. The second theory holds that the scope and scale of the changes will prove so disruptive that many banks will find themselves scrambling to catch up, or, worse, will be unable to compete in a mobile-enabled landscape.

"Some people believe that banks will adapt to mobile in the same way that they adapted to previous disruptive forces such as call centers, ATMs, and the Internet," says Chris. "But those were evolutionary changes in technology. Today's disruptions are more fundamental. The mobile Internet represents more than just new technology. It's connecting everyone on the planet."

Essentially, the mobile Internet is creating a global community of highly empowered consumers. Suddenly, after centuries of being the underdog, the consumer is at the top of the mountain!

"That is a huge difference and banks will not simply *evolve* to a new business model that keeps pace with the market. Banks will have to *disrupt* to the new model. Banks that try to adapt and evolve will end up as losers, because the changes occurring are fundamental and fast," says Chris.

The only salvation for banks that hope to *evolve* rather than to *disrupt* will be their banking licenses, says Chris. By the way, Chris isn't the only expert with this viewpoint. Over the course of researching and writing this book, several sources spoke of banks relying on government regulation as a bulwark against disruptive change. It always strikes me as odd how some banks can rail against regulation when it seems inconvenient and then embrace it when it works in their favor!

In my conversation with Chris, he suggested that the world is ready for a new kind of financial institution. Traditional banks, he says, spent decades and untold millions of dollars integrating the services they offered. This integration wasn't done for the benefit of bank customers—it was done to make it more difficult for a bank's customers to switch their accounts to a rival bank.

The advent of mobile technology makes it possible for bank services to become "de-constituted," as Chris says, back into separate offerings that consumers would access through various apps on the mobile devices. In a very real sense, the integrated bank model would dissolve (or disintegrate) and be replaced by an atomized model empowering consumers to assemble highly customized "virtual banks" at will on their mobile devices.

No wonder some bankers are frightened. When you look into the future through the eyes of someone like Chris, you clearly see a world of empowered consumers. What you don't see is a world of empowered banks.

Why Innovation Is Foundational

Let's return for a moment to the concept of innovation. Thanks to relentless overuse, the word *innovation* has lost much of its punch. It has joined a pantheon of great words, such as *paradigm* and *revolution*, that have been beaten into submission by merciless marketers and craven copywriters.

For a moment, let's pretend that the word *innovation* still packs a wallop and commands your attention. For me, this is an easy exercise. All I have to do is pick up my dog-eared paperback copy of *The Innovator's Dilemma* by Clayton M. Christensen.

Christensen reminds us that innovation is still a powerful concept. He accomplishes that feat by showing us what happens to companies that don't take innovation seriously. They stumble. They lose money. They fail. The book is simultaneously frightening, exciting, and inspiring.

One of Christensen's main points is that disruptive innovations often seem, at least initially, to be irrational investments.

> *First, disruptive products are simpler and cheaper; they generally promise lower margins, not greater profits. Second,*

disruptive technologies typically are first commercialized in emerging or insignificant markets. And third, leading firms' most profitable customers generally don't want, and indeed initially can't use, products based on disruptive technologies. By and large, a disruptive technology is initially embraced by the least profitable customers in a market.[14]

Christensen takes pains to emphasize how disruptive innovations deviate from common sense and traditional business acumen—which is why successful companies often ignore or dismiss critical innovations (e.g., Xerox not seeing the business potential of the computer mouse it had invented).

In many instances, innovation blindness is self-inflicted. It's standard practice for companies to concentrate on satisfying the needs and desires of their most profitable customers. But as Christensen pointedly observes, focusing on your most profitable customers can blind you to the needs and potential value of other customer groups that are less profitable. The dilemma arises when someone in your organization comes up with an innovation that might be perfect for addressing the needs of a customer group that isn't your most profitable group.

We all know the saying, "If it ain't broke, don't fix it." Sadly, that saying has been used to justify the strangling of many new ideas. For the decision makers at Xerox, the computer mouse seemed irrelevant to their corporate sales strategy. Apparently, no one made a serious effort to identify another group of customers to whom the mouse would appeal. It took the genius of Steve Jobs to perceive the mouse's appeal, and to commercialize it.

There are times, according to Christensen, when it is proper to invest in products that promise, at least initially, to deliver lower margins than established products, and there are times when it makes sense to explore developing markets in which new customers might be less profitable—again, initially—than existing customers in established markets.

"Products based on disruptive technologies are typically cheaper, simpler, smaller, and frequently more convenient to use," writes Christensen. Wow, it sounds to me like he's describing a mobile banking app. It's certainly cheaper, smaller, and more convenient than setting up a new branch office for your bank!

Mobile banking can also be developed through reverse innovation, which refers to a process of developing, testing, refining, and marketing low-cost products in underdeveloped economies such as China or India, and then distributing them in other markets across the world.[15] It's called "reverse innovation" because it reverses the traditional approach to product development, which typically produces a high-cost full-feature version for developed economies, followed by a low-cost no-frills version for undeveloped economies.

Reverse innovation strategies have been used successfully by companies such as GE, Procter & Gamble, and Microsoft. Essentially, reverse innovation recognizes that some forms of innovation occur more quickly in undeveloped or developing economies, where the need to innovate is driven by the lack of resources and other constraints.

The net takeaway is that in fast-moving competitive markets, innovation is critical to both survival and success. There is no substitute for continuous innovation and improvement; in modern economies, they are absolutely essential. Without innovation, you are standing still, which is the same as moving backward.

I'll say it again: Innovate or die. The choice is crystal clear and unambiguous. If you choose innovation, this book is for you. If the idea of innovation frightens you, put the book down and leave by one of the emergency exits. As Alec Baldwin's character famously asks at the beginning of *Glengarry Glen Ross*, "Have I got your attention now?"[15]

Notes

1. www.mckinsey.it/storage/first/uploadfile/attach/139854/file/trin07.pdf
2. http://management.fortune.cnn.com/2013/11/21/marc-andreessen/
3. www.itu.int/en/ITU-D/Statistics/Documents/facts/ICTFacts-Figures2013.pdf
4. www.portioresearch.com/media/3986/Portio%20Research%20Mobile%20Factbook%202013.pdf
5. http://africacenter.org/wp-content/uploads/2013/10/ARP5-Africas-Information-Revolution1.pdf
6. http://sites.duke.edu/marx/category/telecom/special-access/
7. http://mobithinking.com/mobile-marketing-tools/latest-mobile-stats/a#subscribers
8. www.gatesfoundation.org/What-We-Do/Global-Development/Financial-Services-for-the-Poor
9. http://docs.gatesfoundation.org/Documents/Fighting%20Poverty%20Profitably%20Full%20Report.pdf
10. www.partnershiptoendpoverty.org/unbankedwhitepaper.pdf
11. The article was expanded into a book, *The Fortune at the Bottom of the Pyramid: Eradicating Poverty through Profits* (Upper Saddle River, NJ: Prentice Hall, 2004).
12. Peter H. Diamandis and Steven Kotler, *Abundance: The Future Is Better Than You Think* (New York: Free Press, 2012).
13. Chris Skinner, *Digital Bank: Strategies to Succeed as a Digital Bank* (CreateSpace Independent Publishing Platform; Kent, UK: Financial Services Club, 2013).
14. Clayton M. Christensen, *The Innovator's Dilemma: The Revolutionary Book That Will Change the Way You Do Business* (Boston: Harvard Business School Press, 1997; New York: HarperBusiness, 2011).
15. www.youtube.com/watch?v=8kZg_ALxEz0

CHAPTER 2

How Did We Get Here?

A Rich History, with Lots of Luggage

As mentioned earlier, banking dates back to the second millennium BC, although there is evidence suggesting that banking could be much older. The first banks were probably royal granaries. They were built to collect, store, and distribute a kingdom's surplus grain. They also lent grain, apparently to farmers and traders.

Modern banking began in Renaissance Italy and spread gradually across Europe. Early banking centers included Florence, Hamburg, Amsterdam, and London. The first central bank, the Bank of London, was founded in 1694. The U.S. Federal Reserve was created in 1913, and the European Central Bank was created in 1998. By the time you read this, the world's most important bank might be the People's Bank of China in Beijing.

Banks have come a long way since the dawn of commerce, and the story of banking is still unfolding. Despite the passage of time, however, the basics of banking have remained surprisingly unchanged. Here's a brief definition of banking from the 10th edition of *Principles of Money, Banking & Financial Markets*:

> *Banks provide a place where individuals and businesses can invest their funds to earn interest at a minimum of risk. Banks, in turn, redeploy these funds by making loans.*[1]

It doesn't get much simpler than that. As we know, however, banks also serve an important role in maintaining a nation's money supply. Banks also create money by using their excess reserves to issue loans. In a very real sense, the issuance of loans creates money, which is why banking often seems magical to people outside the industry.

I mention this because the rise of mobile banking will undoubtedly lead to expectations (and disappointments) over the role of mobile banks in creating money and protecting its value.

Let's pause for a few minutes and talk about money. As we know, but often tend to forget, money did not spring into existence overnight. Money has evolved steadily over time. Sometimes it almost seems as though money has a mercurial or protean quality. Far from being something rock steady and unchangeable, money is a shape-shifter. The purpose of money, as we know, is to reduce the costs and difficulties associated with trade. Trade is essential to almost every culture, and money makes large-scale trade practical.

Before money, trade was conducted through barter, which can be cumbersome and inexact. Barter can be a disincentive to trade since it's hard to assign precise values to whatever it is that you're bartering. Since trade is a prerequisite for specialization and specialization is a prerequisite for economic growth, something better than barter was required.

That something was money. The earliest forms of money included cowrie shells, chunks of obsidian, oxen, cow manure, pressed tablets of salt, and bricks of tea. Unlike our present-day money, so-called commodity money had both abstract and intrinsic value. But not everyone always agreed on the precise value of commodity money, so it wasn't an ideal medium of exchange.

Eventually, commodity money was replaced by coined money, which was more portable and more widely accepted in trade for the simple reason that almost anyone could immediately grasp the value of a coin minted from easily recognizable metals such as gold, silver, bronze, or copper.

Paper money was the next step on the evolutionary staircase. Paper money began as warehouse receipts given in exchange for deposits of gold or metal coins. It didn't take long for people to realize that they could use the receipts themselves to pay for items they wanted to purchase. It also didn't take the warehouse owners long to figure out that they could make loans by simply issuing new warehouse receipts. In effect, they were creating money.

The money we use today is referred to as "fiat money," since it has no intrinsic value and it is not tied to a precious metal such as gold. Today's money has value because the government says it has value, and we, as a society, agree to go along. Modern money symbolizes the social contract that we have cobbled together over the millennia. It serves multiple duties as an easy means of payment, a handy way to store value, and a recognizable standard unit of value.

We all complain about money, but it's one of humankind's greatest and noblest inventions. It represents a bond of trust, often among strangers. Without money, it's hard to imagine any kind of modern civilization. When you find yourself questioning the value of today's money, ask yourself if you would really want to live in the world where the primary medium of exchange was cow manure.

I think that we can agree that money is continuously evolving, and that it reflects the evolving nature of a larger social contract that allows most of us to live together in a state of relative peace, safety, and mutual trust. That being said, it's fair to wonder about the future of money. Based on our knowledge of the past, it seems likely that money will evolve to keep pace with the digital economy. But there are many unanswered questions, such as:

- What form will money take?
- What role it will play in our increasingly networked society?

- Which institutions will be responsible for maintaining and controlling the money supply?
- Will money remain the primary means of payment, or will something else replace it?

Is Mobile Banking a Real Trend?

I would argue that mobile banking is a growing trend with a bright future. According to PwC Research, mobile will dethrone branch networks as a dominant channel of customer interaction with financial institutions.[2] Mobile is expected to unseat personal computers (PCs) as the preferred mode of Internet access by 2015. In the United States, the number of mobile banking customers is expected to reach 77 million by 2014. Clearly, mobile banking is surging.

The Reserve Bank of India reports that 13 million people in India used mobile banking services in fiscal year 2012. A total of 25.6 million transactions valued at Rs. 1,820 crore occurred, involving 59 banks, a growth of 198 percent and 174 percent in volume and value terms, respectively, compared to the previous year.

In addition to being more convenient for customers, mobile banking represents a low-cost channel for retail banks. Branches, call centers, and ATMs are expensive investments relative to the costs of mobile banking.

It's All about Location

Traditional retail banking, online banking, and mobile banking differ primarily in where they occur. Traditional retail banking takes place in a branch office or at an ATM. Online banking is conducted on a PC or tablet. Mobile banking is done on a mobile phone or mobile-enabled tablet.

To be fair, mobile banking is a work in progress, and only time will tell. Are mobile banks merely incorporeal versions of traditional banks, or are they something else? What role will pure-play mobile banks have in the new financial landscape, and how will they be regulated? Or perhaps a better question is *who* will regulate them?

Mobile banking is likely to change the way we think about money. Mobile phones are rapidly morphing into the mobile wallets, which means that we will be carrying less money (and less loose change) in our pockets and pocketbooks. Gradually over the next two or three years, we will use our mobile phones for an increasingly greater percentage of our financial transactions.

Very soon, all of our smaller, daily, or routine purchases— train tickets, coffee, breakfast, chewing gum, breath mints, lottery tickets, bread, milk, chips, drinks after work, movie tickets, dry cleaning, feeding the parking meter—will be handled through our mobile phones or tablets. I cannot promise you that we will discard our wallets and purses entirely, but they are likely to become much smaller.

Let's take a quick look at the difference between mobile banking and mobile banks. For the most part, mobile banking is essentially a digital extension of traditional banking. Behind the electronic curtain is a traditional bank with branch offices.

A mobile bank, however, is a horse of a different color. A mobile bank exists for the purpose of enabling mobile transactions. You would never go into a branch office of a mobile bank because there are no branch offices. (I should never say "never," though, because it's possible that a successful mobile bank might decide to extend its business into the physical world by opening branch offices.)

At this point, it seems logical to wonder if mobile banks might eventually replace traditional retail banks. I suppose that scenario is possible, but it's unlikely. Even in an age of digital banking and digital money, there will still be a need for traditional banks.

A major ingredient of successful banking is trust, which is something the big bank brands already have. Mobile banks and other types of nonbanks offering banking services would have to build similar levels of trust before they could seriously threaten traditional banks. Also, banks do more than just cash checks—they create money, they act as caretakers for money, and they enable the commerce that supports our economies. So the short answer is that banks aren't going to vanish tomorrow.

Here's what I do foresee: Traditional banks will do less and less of what they have done traditionally, and nonbanks will do more and more of what traditional banks do now. Eventually, some kind of equilibrium will emerge, and then we'll have a new status quo. Until then, however, it would be wise for traditional banks to view mobile banking as what it is: a highly disruptive innovation requiring careful attention.

Traditional banks that dismiss mobile banking as a fad are making a potentially fatal mistake. Frost & Sullivan research predicts that 45 million U.S. banking customers will be using mobile banking apps by 2014. There is no safe way to ignore the preference of that many customers.

As more millennials and digital natives enter the workforce and become full-fledged contributors to the economy, mobile banking is going to look less like an optional feature and more like a must-have.

My hunch is that fairly soon, all banks will offer some degree of mobile service. At minimum, all banking customers will have the option of downloading two kinds of apps from their bank: an information app and a transaction app. The information app will provide account balance information, as well as updated information about bank products and interest rates. The transaction app will provide essential retail banking services such as check deposit, paying merchants, and transferring money from one account to another. For consumers, mobile banking will translate into greater control of their money.

Banks will compete on the quality, usability, speed, and appearance of their apps. Mobile banking will become a key competitive factor in marketing, customer acquisition, and customer retention.

The world's larger banks (and some smaller ones, too) have already seen the future, and they're moving in the direction of accommodating the needs of the younger generation. There is also a new breed of start-ups such as Moven, Simple, and Green Dot, which technically are not banks but operate in a space that seems a lot like retail banking.

How Free Is Free?

For banks, getting from here to there will certainly entail costs and require investments in new technology and security. But the good news is that the mobile service providers and mobile network operators have already done much of the heavy lifting. Banks won't get a free ride, but they won't have to build the basic infrastructure necessary to make mobile banking systems work.

The same conditions apply to other parts of the financial services sector that see the competitive advantages inherent in mobile strategies. Insurers such as the Government Employees Insurance Company (GEICO) and Allstate have already staked claims in the mobile marketplace, providing customers with highly usable and visually appealing mobile apps. You can bet that more companies will follow in their footsteps.

M-Payments

For the present, the main reason for mobile banking is the ability to make mobile payments (m-payments) from your mobile device. Worldwide, m-payments are growing strongly, but still represent a fraction of e-commerce payments. Here are some key data points:

- Merchandise purchases (e.g., purchasing via Amazon and eBay) account for most of m-payments in developed markets.
- Money transfers and prepaid top-ups account for most of m-payments. Travel ticketing and parking are also expected to be popular in developing markets.
- Gartner predicts that in 2016 there will be 448 million m-payment users, in a market worth $617 billion. The Asia-Pacific region will have the most m-payment users, but Africa will account for the highest revenues.
- Mobile web is expected to dominate mobile payments in North America and Europe through to 2016. Short message service (SMS), or texting, is expected to remain the key vehicle for m-payments in developing markets. Near field communications (NFC) transactions will remain relatively low through 2015, but will start to pick up in 2016.
- Yankee Group predicts that global mobile transactions will grow to more than $1 trillion by 2015.
- Europe, the Middle East, and Africa (EMEA) is the mobile money hot spot, says Yankee, accounting for 41 percent of mobile transactions value in 2011, compared to 35 percent in North America, 22 percent in the Asia-Pacific region, and just 1 percent in Latin America.
- Portio Research estimates that by the end of 2014, nearly 490 million people worldwide (8 percent of mobile sub-scribers) will be using their mobile devices to make payments (including in-app payments, mobile ticketing, and mobile coupons).
- Juniper Research predicts that total value of mobile payments for digital and physical goods, money transfers, and NFC transactions will reach $670 billion by 2015. This

amount includes mobile ticketing, NFC contactless payments, physical goods purchases, and money transfers. Active mobile money users will double by 2013. Digital goods is the largest segment and will account for nearly 40 percent of the market in 2015.

- Juniper Research also projects that 2.5 billion consumers worldwide will buy digital goods via their mobile devices in 2015. More than 400 million people on the Indian subcontinent will purchase digital goods via mobile in 2015.
- But IDC believes that in EMEA, m-payments will take off more slowly than m-banking, forecasting that less than 13 percent of mobile subscribers will be registered to use m-payments and the volume of m-payments will be no more than $125 billion. Thus m-payments will begin more slowly than many industry observers hope, due to the complexity and setup costs for retailers. However, strong growth in m-banking will lay the foundations for growth in mobile payments.
- Money transfer and merchandise are expected to be the biggest contributors, accounting for 69 percent and 23 percent, respectively, of the total transactional value.
- In 2012, Africa was the largest region by transaction value with some $60 billion in mobile payment transactions. In 2017, the Asia-Pacific region is expected to be the largest market, surpassing Africa with approximately $205 billion in mobile payment transactions.
- The user base of the global mobile payment market is expected to cross 450 million, with a transaction value of more than $721 billion by 2017, a compound annual growth rate (CAGR) of 18 percent and 35 percent, respectively, between 2012 and 2017.
- The Middle East and Latin America are expected to grow at the fastest pace, clocking a CAGR growth of 82 percent and 78 percent, respectively, between 2012 and 2017.

Creating the Future of Mobile Banking

I hope that you have enjoyed what you have read so far, and I urge you to stay with me. Together, we will explore the emerging mobile economy and its many interlocking components. Many questions remain; I will attempt to provide enough information in the subsequent chapters of this book to satisfy your professional interest and personal curiosity.

I may not have all the answers, but one thing I know for certain is that mobile banking is innovation incarnate. It is young, fresh, and new. There are no traditions to overturn, and no legacy systems to work around. The future of mobile banking is a clean slate; its history is being written now.

All of us with a stake in the future of financial services need to learn as much as we can about mobile banking and its various cousins. This book is designed to serve as a resource for you and your colleagues as we—our society and our industry—move forward into the exciting future of mobile banking and mobile financial services.

Another observation before moving on: It's often said that money is the root of all evil. I have seen with my own eyes that the opposite is true. Money is a tool—or a system, if you will; it enables the creation of vast wealth, which, in turn, lifts and enriches the lives of millions of people—not merely in the material sense, but in the spiritual sense as well.

Each step in the evolution of money—from barter to commodity money to coins to paper—has resulted in the creation of more wealth and generated more happiness for greater numbers of people. The latest step, the emergence of digital money, will provide even more benefits to even greater numbers of people, and especially to those living in parts of the world where there are currently few banks or financial institutions.

I am not so naive as to believe that money in itself can buy happiness, but I firmly believe that money can provide a path to happiness. If I did not believe that, I would not have become a banker.

Notes

1. Lawrence S. Ritter and William L. Silber, *Principles of Money, Banking & Financial Markets*, 10th ed. (New York: Basic Books, 1986).
2. PricewaterhouseCooper. "The new digital tipping point." 2011. Available at http://www.pwc.com/en_GX/gx/banking-capital-markets/publications/assets/pdf/Primed_for_the_digi_tipping_point_Layout_3-1.pdf.

CHAPTER 3

Welcome to Generation M

"See and Hear" Replacing "Touch and Smell"

Now is the proper time to check in with my good friend Brett King. Many of you have heard of Brett's company, Moven, which is essentially a mobile bank. I asked Brett why he decided to launch a mobile bank and why he thinks the timing for such a venture might be just right.

I was a little surprised when Brett did not begin his answer with a discussion of banking per se. Instead, he spoke at length about the differences between baby boomers or Gen Xers and the millennials of Generation Y or digital natives of Generation Z.

Brett refers to this new demographic as Generation M. From Brett's point of view, the *M* doesn't stand for *millennial*. It stands for *mobile*.

Let me share with you some quotes from Brett's blog on the *Huffington Post*:

> *Baby Boomers and Gen-X have in common the need to experience life in all its glory. Whether that is born out of a sense of adventure, the need for tactile feedback or in the sense of face-to-face social connections, at the core of much of our buying behavior historically has been the need to "touch and feel" a product before a purchase. There's a subtle shift*

in this behavior with Gen-Y and Gen-Z/Digital Natives (sometimes collectively called Generation-M or, as Time Magazine *called them, the "multi-tasking" generation) that is critical to understand if you are going to engage this community successfully moving forward, and it emphasizes why the physical store is under increased threat.*[1]

I love how Brett notes "the need for tactile feedback." It reminds me of when I was shopping for my first car. I remember telling a friend that I was going to the showroom to "kick the tires." That seems so old-fashioned now, doesn't it? But that's how we were brought up—we needed that face-to-face experience. We needed to smell the distinct odor of a new car interior before we closed the deal.

As Brett correctly observes, however, the psychology of buying has undergone a dramatic transformation. That transformation isn't limited to automobiles. It's widespread, across the entire retail sector, including banks. Here's another quote from Brett's blog:

In the banking space, I'm often confronted with passionate arguments for why face-to-face interactions, the availability of advice and the psychological comfort of brick-and-mortar spaces still matter. The problem is that those describing these "values" are inevitably Baby Boomers or Gen-X consumers, describing their comfort levels and buying behaviors. There are a number of key trends we can observe today that signify an abandonment of this traditional buying behavior for the next generation of customers.

If I understand Brett correctly, the old paradigm of "touch and smell" has been replaced by a new paradigm of "see and hear." I am not using the word *paradigm* lightly. We have experienced nothing less than a sea change in buying habits. Much of the past has been washed away, as if by a storm of immense proportions. What remains is something new and somewhat unexpected. As bankers, we need to get over our collective shock and accept the fact that the world around us has changed.

Here's a great story that Brett tells to illustrate the point:

I recently asked my 13-year-old daughter how she would send a small amount of money to her friend Tia in London. Without hesitation, she said she would text the money to her. If for some reason texting didn't work, she would send the money by email, she said. When I explained that she would need to write her friend a check and put it in the regular mail, she laughed and said, "Daddy, don't be silly. No one would ever do that." Clearly, she thought that I had lost my mind.

I am sure that my daughter has seen my checkbook lying around. But I do not believe that she connects it with money, or that she thinks that it serves any practical purpose in our lives.

From the mouths of babes comes wisdom. It seems as though we have a choice: We can train our kids to write checks, or we can enable their mobile phones to perform similar tasks. Personally, I think it will be far easier to program a new generation of mobile devices to perform financial transactions than it will be to train a new generation of human beings to write checks, balance their checkbooks, calculate compound interest rates, choose the most appropriate financial instruments, and make hundreds of informed decisions about their money while possessing only a superficial knowledge of incredibly complex financial systems. That is just my opinion, of course.

Taking the Friction Out

From Brett's perspective, the value of mobile banking is that it makes it easier for us to buy things. It accomplishes this feat by stripping or reducing friction from purchase processes. Let's take an example that we're all likely to find familiar.

You need a new car. You go to the dealership, choose a car, and sit down with a sales associate to make a deal. The associate asks you if you plan to finance the car. Unless you have brought a suitcase full of cash or a certified check for the full price of the car (plus fees and taxes) with you, your answer will be "yes."

Twenty years ago, answering "yes" would have required you to visit a bank branch, apply for a car loan, fill out a lengthy paper application, and wait for the loan to be approved. Only then could you go back to the dealership and pick up the car.

Today, the loan application process begins the moment after you say "yes." While you are sipping coffee, tea, or soda, the dealership's finance team is putting together a loan for you. If your credit score is acceptable, you will drive away with your brand-new car within a few hours.

Now, imagine doing all of that on your mobile phone. Two or three years from now—possibly sooner—you won't even have to sit down with a sales associate at the dealership. An app on your mobile phone will handle the entire process of buying the car and obtaining the loan. All you'll need is a ride to the dealership to pick up the car.

That's what Brett means when he talks about removing friction from the purchase process.

"Nobody *needs* a mortgage, a car loan, a checking account, or a credit card," says Brett. "We go through the motions of applying for loans and obtaining credit so we can purchase the goods and services that we need or desire. Our objective is making the purchase."

Applying for a loan, writing a check, or even swiping a credit card adds friction to the buying process. The more friction you add, the less likely it is that people will buy. Reducing friction, in contrast, makes it easier for people to buy what they want, when they want it.

Uber, for example, is a service that uses a mobile app to connect riders and drivers in 35 cities. You tap the app and you order a taxicab. The payment capability is built into the app. You don't have to swipe a card or exchange cash with the driver.

"You get what you want—a cab ride," says Brett. "The financial transaction is almost completely invisible and seamless."

Services such as Uber offer glimpses into our future as a cash-free society. Remember, money is a tool. It's a way of getting from point A to point B. Money is not a destination; it's merely a vehicle.

In Chapter 2, we looked briefly at the evolution of money, and we saw how money is the really the key factor in developing a successful economy. Physical forms of money—commodity money, metal money, and even paper money—are inherently inconvenient and risky to transport. Back in the days when you had to lug three or four bags of metal coins to the market, you were less likely to saddle up your donkey and make the trip. As a result, the economy of your town suffered.

I look at mobile banking and mobile finance as logical stages in the evolution of money. To my eyes, what's exciting about mobile banking isn't the technology; what's exciting is how mobile banking enables consumers to make purchases more easily and more safely than ever before.

Mobile Operators and Banking

The emerging ecosystem of mobile banking is a fascinating convergence of telecoms, retailers, and financial services organizations. Oddly enough, however, today's leaders in the mobile banking field are telecoms, not banks. To a certain extent, the idea of telecoms leading the way makes sense, because they have the technical expertise and, quite literally, the bandwidth to get the job done—at least in the short term.

Isis in the United States and Project Oscar in the United Kingdom are examples of combined efforts by telecoms to provide mobile payment services. Isis is a joint venture of AT&T, T-Mobile, and Verizon Wireless and relies on near field communications (NFC) technology. Project Oscar is a mobile wallet joint venture among Everything Everywhere, O2, and VodaFone. Oscar relies on radio frequency identification (RFID) to enable mobile transactions.

M-Pesa, launched by Safaricom and VodaFone in 2007 in Kenya, has 30,000 agents and 14 million users. About 70 percent of all electronic transfers in Kenya—roughly $1 billion per month—are done through M-Pesa, making it a leader in the mobile banking space.

SMART Money is an electronic wallet initiative of Smart Communications, the leading mobile service provider in the Philippines. SMART Money is connected to 12 partner banks and can be used for transactions at 9,000 ATMs nationwide. It can be used to transfer funds, pay bills, and reload airtime. Here's a cool feature: You can use SMART Money to send funds to any of Smart Communications' 50.9 million subscribers, anywhere in the Philippines. From my perspective, that is a low-friction system!

Retailers are also climbing onto the bandwagon. Starbucks, Wal-Mart, and Home Depot are experimenting with mobile payment apps such as Square's mobile wallet and PayPal's in-store checkout.

Top U.S. retailers such as Wal-Mart, Phillips 66, Gap, 7-Eleven, Best Buy, Target, and Dunkin' Donuts have formed a company called Merchant Customer Exchange (MCX), a mobile payment network that allows its customers to pay by mobile phone application at participating retail stores, supermarkets, restaurants, and gas stations. MCX says it operates in nearly 90,000 stores and processes more than $1 trillion in payments annually.

Mobile Banks

Simple, GoBank, and Moven are examples of the next wave of mobile banking. Essentially, they are banks that exist for the express purpose of serving mobile customers.

Simple (formerly BankSimple) is a privately owned company founded in 2009 and headquartered in Portland, Oregon. Its partners include Visa, Bancorp Bank, Allpoint, TxVia, Cachet, and CPI Financial. Simple provides banking services to more than 40,000 customers across the United States. It has a nice user interface, clearly designed with younger customers in mind.

GoBank is a brand of Green Dot Bank, launched by Green Dot, a publicly traded bank holding company. GoBank has a modern, user-friendly interface that looks appealing to mobile customers. GoBank also offers features enabling customers to send money via e-mail or Facebook. Clearly, banks such as Simple and GoBank have made the effort to understand their potential market and to deliver services that mobile customers will value and appreciate.

Moven, which is the brainchild of Brett King, was founded on two principal ideas. The first is that mobile communications will fundamentally change the ways in which retail banks operate. The second and perhaps more controversial idea is that the mobile interface can be engineered to offer the same (or better) level of service as is available at a branch office.

Moven enables customers to make payments through a debit card account, receive real-time updates on account status, and access cash through 40,000 surcharge-free ATMs. It also helps customers analyze their spending patterns through two features, MoneyPulse and MoneyPath, which present colorful graphic representations of payments over time.

According to Moven's website, its mission is helping customers become more mindful of their spending so they can achieve their financial goals, enable customers to track spending with easy tools and see their progress over time (so they can stay motivated and keep on track), and access a user-friendly dashboard "with a snapshot of your spending and a full picture of your finances across all of your bank and credit card accounts."

Each time you buy something from a particular merchant, Moven sends you a notification, along with a quick summary of how much you've already spent with that merchant and how much you've spent on that category of purchases.

"Let's say you buy a latte at a coffee shop," Brett explains. "You will see how much you've spent at that shop and how much you've spent on coffee. Real-time information like that can have a huge impact on your spending habits by raising your awareness of how you're actually spending your money."

In some respects, Moven is pushing the traditional boundaries of retail banking by offering a service that seems perfectly suited to the needs of millennials. I can't help but think that Moven's push in that direction is somehow motivated by its market research, which suggested that many millennials desperately need rudimentary money-management services. The research showed that despite their sophisticated use of technology, millennials appear to lack some of the basic money-management skills of previous generations.

Rather than casting stones or assigning blame, Moven is tackling the problem head-on by offering needed services, in a format that millennials feel comfortable using. To me, this represents a perfect example of finding a business opportunity in a challenge. Or as we used to say in Madras, "When you have lemons, make lemonade."

Artifacts for a New Age of Banking

From Brett's perspective, mobile banking services such as those provided by Moven are direct descendants of previous artifacts of retail bank accounts.

"Think of it this way: In the 1950s and 1960s, you had a passbook. In the 1970s and 1980s, you had a checkbook. In the 1990s and first decade of the new century, you had your ATM card," says Brett. "Today, all of those 'artifacts' are being replaced by the mobile phone."

While it might seem to some that mobile banking represents a further abstraction of once-familiar banking services, many younger customers would likely see it as a more tangible representation of their relationship with a financial services provider.

I would argue that from the perspective of a millennial customer, the mobile phone is a more concrete artifact of a relationship with a bank than a passbook, a checkbook, or even an ATM card.

The evolution of financial artifacts and the shifting perceptions of what is abstract and what is concrete are an ongoing process. Paper money seems real to us because we intuitively recognize its value and we accept it as a medium of exchange. We can only guess what a Neanderthal or Cro-Magnon would make of paper money. I suppose they might use it as kindling for their fires.

I can still remember the first time I heard about synthetic derivatives. They seemed totally abstract to me. Twenty years later, we tend to take derivatives for granted. We accept them as legitimate financial instruments, and in our minds, we assign them concrete values.

Thus the debate over what is abstract and what is concrete continues. My hunch is that five years from now, mobile banking will seem just as real to millennials as traditional banking seems to baby boomers and Gen Xers.

Welcome to Generation M—the generation that grew up with mobile phones and tablets. If we, as bankers, do not provide banking services to them on their favorite devices, someone else surely will.

Note

1. www.huffingtonpost.com/brett-king/generation-m-see-and-hear_b_1946776.html

CHAPTER 4

Less Cash, More Sales, Fewer Hassles

Soon, Everyone Will Accept Credit Cards

I think there's a general sense of agreement that the widespread use of credit cards has been a great blessing to the consumer economy. Not having to reach deeper into your wallet or purse to find an extra couple of dollars can make all the difference between making an impulse purchase and walking away. Using credit cards does more than merely increase the likelihood of buying something you desire—it also increases the number of things you will buy and, consequently, the amount of money you spend per shopping trip.

So on a purely theoretical basis, merchants should love credit cards. But many merchants hate them. Here's why: Every time a merchant swipes a credit card, the credit card company takes a cut of the action. Until recently, the credit card companies had the leverage to set their fees at whatever level they wished. The advent of mobile technologies that allow practically any merchant—or any individual, for that matter—to take a credit card have created a new climate of competition and innovation. As a result, many merchants that in the past would have run away from the idea of accepting credit cards are now racing to embrace them.

Phillip M. Miller is Global Head of the Acquirer Knowledge Center at MasterCard. In essence, his role is helping the company expand the universe of merchants who accept MasterCard. From his perspective, mobile is definitely a good thing.

"Today, mobile technology is driving the adoption of credit cards by merchants who had not been willing or able to take them in the past," says Phillip. A new generation of mobile payment technologies makes it far easier for merchants to accept credit cards. All you need is a smartphone with a card reader and the right mobile app, and you're ready to take credit cards.

"Lots of consumers carry credit cards, and they want to be able to use them wherever they shop," says Phillip. "But smaller merchants don't want the hassle of bulky machines and cumbersome processes. As more merchants understand the capabilities offered by smart phones and mobile devices, they are getting more comfortable with the idea of accepting credit cards for large and small transactions."

The proliferation of mobile payment options will have a huge impact on the consumer space. At present, approximately 15 percent of global transactions are made with credit cards. The remaining 85 percent are made with cash, by check, or through Automated Clearing House (ACH) transfers.

Companies like MasterCard, Visa, and American Express see a potential bonanza in the adoption of mobile payment technologies by small merchants. From the perspective of the electronic payments card companies, it represents an amazing opportunity for shifting trillions of dollars in purchases from cash, checking, and ACH to credit, debit, and prepaid cards.

"For merchants, transacting in cash can be expensive. You have to secure it. It can be misplaced or stolen. Accepting cards means that you can reduce those costs," says Phillip.

It also represents a potential boon for smaller merchants who rely on impulse purchases to generate revenue. "Merchants who accept cards actually get a higher average ticket, because a consumer who buys only one or two items based on the cash in their pockets can now buy three or four items with a card," says Phillip. "Let's say you're at a weekend craft fair and you see something you want to buy. Some of those handmade items are expensive, and you might not have the cash in your pocket to make the purchase. If the seller can process your credit or debit card on a mobile device, everybody wins."

Will the proliferation of mobile payments lead to the demise of the checkbook? Yes, probably. As Phillip notes, many of us tend to use our checkbooks when paying for services such as gardening, housekeeping, and trash hauling. "At some point, the gardener is going to take credit cards because it's less hassle for him and he won't have to worry about depositing and keeping track of checks," says Phillip. "Checking is expensive for the banks, too."

As a banker, I agree. Processing checks is expensive, and most banks would be happy to exit the checking business.

Electronic payment cards will also be helpful in emerging economies, where cash is used almost exclusively outside of urban areas. Credit and debit cards are less easily stolen and are easier to track. Card transactions leave a trail that can be audited, when necessary. The ability to track and audit card transactions has many upsides, including reduced fraud, faster deposits of funds, and increased tax revenue for local governments since it's harder to hide credit and debit card transactions than cash transactions!

Following the Path to Acceptance

Banesh Prabhu is Senior Executive Vice President and Group Head of Technology and Operations at Siam Commercial Bank in Thailand. A former colleague of mine, he has held several top posts at Citibank, including Global Operations Head of Citibank's

Global Consumer Group–International. I asked him recently to describe his views on the impact of mobile technology on our industry. His replies were instructive and illuminating.

"From a customer-facing perspective, I believe that mobile banking is actually overtaking web-based banking in many areas, particularly with the mass segments," says Banesh. "The biggest opportunities are in mobile payments. More and more banking activities are taking place on mobile devices."

Banesh lists four types of payments in which mobile is surging:

1. Direct payment by a consumer to a merchant for a purchase, usually using a bank account without a card
2. People-to-people payments
3. Top-up payments such as E-ZPass, mobile
4. Bill payments to merchants (e.g., utility bills, mortgage payments)

Looking at mobile payments through Banesh's eyes reveals an entirely new universe of opportunities for banks that are willing to make the right investments in the people, processes, and technologies required to implement and support mobile platforms.

Banesh also sees growing opportunities for banks to offer consumer-friendly informational services to their customers via their mobile devices. Mobile will also accelerate the continuing growth of e-commerce, which opens up many new and potentially profitable ways for banks to engage consumers.

That said, Banesh strongly suggests that banks aim for "channel efficiency," by which he means that banks should strive to offer the best possible customer experiences at the lowest possible costs via the mobile channel. "Providing great service at the lowest cost is clearly an objective you want to pursue," says Banesh.

The idea is straightforward: As consumers become more comfortable with the idea of mobile banking, they will tend to favor mobile interactions over in-person interactions for many types of services. As more customers migrate to the mobile channel, banks can spend less money on their branches. Those savings can be invested in developing even better mobile services, creating a win-win situation for banks and their customers.

"Over time, I see mobile driving down unit costs significantly in the mass segment," says Banesh. "In my mind, the strategy is about driving customers to mobile as much as possible, at all levels of banking, from the developing world to the developed economies."

I really like how Banesh focuses on the business case for mobile banking. When I listen to Banesh, it occurs to me that mobile banking is similar to the ATM card—at first, it seemed strange and unusual. Many people resisted using ATM cards, for a wide variety of reasons. Now everyone has an ATM card or something like it. In fact, the ATM card itself is becoming something of a relic, thanks to mobile payments. Like Banesh, I predict that mobile banking is likely to follow a path of gradual acceptance, followed by broad popularity. And then, like the ATM card, it will become increasingly invisible.

CHAPTER 5

Readiness Steps

Making It Real and Taking Your Show on the Road

As Hamlet says to Horatio, "The readiness is all."

In point of fact, Hamlet speaks the line a few minutes before he is poked with a poisoned sword by Ophelia's brother, Laertes, but the heart of his observation is true: Readiness is all.

With that thought in mind, here is the question I pose to anyone considering a mobile banking strategy: Are you ready?

To assist you in answering the question, here is a checklist of readiness steps. When you've checked the boxes, you're good to go!

- ☐ *Step 1: Set your goals.* What's your purpose? Is it driving revenue, lowering costs, protecting an existing market, developing a new market, or simply keeping up with the Joneses?

- ☐ *Step 2: Find out what your market really wants from a mobile banking app.* Follow the timeless advice of genius serial entrepreneur Steve Blank: Get out of the building and talk to customers.

- ☐ *Step 3: Decide whether you're going to build or buy your apps.* Either way, get to know your app developers. Mobile app developers are a new and different breed; you definitely will need to know how to communicate effectively with them.

☐ *Step 4: Prepare for liftoff.* Launching a successful mobile banking service requires more than just developing great apps. You also need to partner and coordinate with the rest of the enterprise: sales, marketing, legal, information technology (IT), finance, operations, and so on. Become an evangelist and promote the service internally. Make sure all of your ducks are lined up before you launch.

☐ *Step 5: Plan to collect data and measure results.* From the moment your service goes live, you must continuously analyze your data and apply the knowledge you acquire to optimize, refine, and improve your offering. That's the only way to stay ahead of the competition.

Look before you leap, be prepared, and don't go off half-cocked. Lay out exactly what you want to achieve with your mobile strategy, and make sure that everyone understands what you're doing.

Get the right players, and start building teams to execute your strategy. In addition to app developers, you will need IT suppliers, integrators, and consultants to make sure that all the technology works together smoothly and seamlessly.

Don't forget about costs and pricing. Typically, mobile is seen as a low-cost channel. But customers should also see it as a preferred channel. Make sure that it delivers truly excellent service and benefits to users, and that it offers real value and unique features.

At the very least—and this is very important—make sure that when you present an existing customer with a form to fill out, most of the fields have been automatically filled in by your system before the customer ever sees it! Seemingly minor services like prepopulated forms go a long way toward building customer loyalty.

Also, always remember that tomorrow will come a lot more quickly than you expect. Make certain that your technology is flexible enough to be easily upgraded, expanded, optimized, and rescaled to meet the changing needs of your market. Build artificial intelligence (AI) into your systems. The Age of Robotics is already upon us, so don't be the only one on the block with no robotic capabilities.

The AI and robotics that you build into the your systems will help you do a better job of keeping pace with the continually evolving needs, whims, and desires of your customers. At a minimum, AI will help you automate your self-service offerings and identify problems before they become major headaches.

Don't forget about back-end integration. Your apps must be seamlessly integrated with the bank's existing systems and subsystems. In other words, the apps cannot be stand-alone offerings. They must be part of a larger whole and fully interoperable within your existing IT architecture.

From the moment you launch until the moment you retire your mobile banking platform (one hopes that will be many years from now), make sure that you are collecting data and closely watching key performance metrics. Don't guess about the performance of your apps and their supporting systems—measure, measure, and measure!

To a certain degree, you will have to treat your mobile banking service as a start-up. That means you won't be able to predict precisely which aspect of the service will be a hit with customers and which will be a miss. Again, just make sure that you have built plenty of flexibility into your plans so you can make course adjustments as you go.

My friends in start-up companies sometimes say they're "always in beta," which is another way of saying they are constantly testing, measuring, and refining their products or services. I fully realize that banks aren't comfortable with the idea of beta releases, but in many circumstances, you just have to go with what you've got. As one of my start-up friends says, "Hope for the best, and prepare for the worst."

Channel Discipline

My friend Jim Marous is a retail banking expert, and he writes *Bank Marketing Strategy*,[1] a great blog that I recommend highly. In a recent conversation about mobile banking, he raised an excellent point that I'd like to share with you. Here's the gist, from my perspective: Banks have developed a tendency to believe that all of their customer-facing channels should be capable of delivering a generally similar set of services to customers. As a result of this mistaken belief, it takes banks far too long to develop capabilities across multiple channels. Essentially, the banks are trying too hard to achieve a goal that isn't necessary.

Not all channels are created equal. Some are more valuable than others. Some channels are great for some kinds of customer interactions, and not so great for other kinds of interactions. Each channel has a bunch of pluses and minuses, strengths and weaknesses, pros and cons.

The takeaway here is to remember that each channel doesn't have to do everything. It would be a critical error to assume that all of your channels have to offer the same range of service and functionality. In fact, the opposite is true. Customers have an intuitive understanding of what their mobile devices can and cannot do.

My advice is to approach your channel strategy as you would approach the task of baking a cake. Yes, it's important to have all the right ingredients at hand, but it's more important to get the proportions right, know when to add ingredients, and know precisely how long to bake the cake.

As Jim notes, some channels—such as mobile—are probably better at handling relatively straightforward transactions that are already in progress. Branches, however, are still probably the best places for resolving more complex issues or initiating certain types of transactions. Another example: As long as people need cash at 2 A.M., there will probably be ATMs. And surveys show that direct mail remains an effective channel for marketing some bank products.

One day, in the not too distant future, the entire mortgage application and approval process will be fully automated and delivered via mobile device. Until that day arrives, however, there will be a need for bank branches and loan officers. I know that Chris Skinner would disagree with me here, but I'm beginning to believe that the shift to mobile banking will be gradual and piecemeal, evolutionary as opposed to revolutionary. That doesn't mean that the change won't be disruptive; it just means that it will occur with less fanfare than some pundits are predicting.

There won't be rioting in the streets—at least I hope there won't be. Our general sense of normalcy won't be greatly shaken or perturbed. We've come to expect a steady pace of change, and that's probably what we'll see as mobile banking takes hold: slow but steady change.

That's why it will be important to maintain a sense of channel discipline. Dramatic gestures and sweeping disruptions are not required to achieve progress. If you try too hard to make every channel do everything perfectly, or if you attempt to load every channel with new and amazing functionality, the resulting mediocrity will only serve to irritate and antagonize your customers. Your channel strategy might look good on a PowerPoint slide, but your customers won't be happy.

Treating Different Channels Differently

I want to stick with the topic of channel strategy a bit longer, because it's important to grasp the interplay and relationships between channels. Mobile and online might seem like similar channels, but they are actually quite different. Each has particular strengths and weaknesses that must be taken into consideration.

I recently interviewed Danny Tang, a channel transformation leader at IBM. Danny has been with Big Blue for 12 years, and he travels around the world advising bank executives on the latest trends. Danny raised several points that I had not fully considered, and I'm grateful for his input. Here are edited excerpts of my excellent conversation with Danny:

Mobile banking has been around now for four or five years, so I no longer have to explain it to people or stress its importance. What we have discovered, though, is that banks are shifting their focus. For a while they were focused mainly on developing and promoting their mobile channel. It was all about educating consumers and signing them up for mobile banking. Now the banks are returning to the idea of improving the customer experience. We need to make mobile banking more attractive and easier to use. We need to add more functionality without adding complexity.

At the same time, the banks are refocusing on improving and refreshing the online banking experience. The refresh cycle for online banking is about five or six years. But think about what was happening five or six years ago: The smartphone revolution hadn't happened. Now it seems like everyone has a smartphone. People have different expectations. User interfaces have changed dramatically, and the old design paradigms aren't as effective.

Today, banks are paying attention to refreshing their online channels. They are developing finger-centric designs that make the online experience more like the mobile experience. They are modernizing their websites to keep pace with today's users.

The research agrees. An Ovum report on 2014 banking trends shows that banks see improving the online channel as their top priority. Improving mobile is the second priority, followed by improving branches. Danny says it's wrong to discount the value of branch banking:

> *Some people believe that branch banking is dead, but that's far from the truth. Banking is an emotional business, and customers need face-to-face contact, especially for the high-end products. The most profitable products still are sold through branches, and that's where the deals are closed. Mobile and online banking are important channels, but they are not the only channels. Branches still play a very important role in the overall picture.*

Danny counsels banks to stay focused on business goals when allocating resources for channel improvements. Banks offer an amazingly wide variety of products and services to a broad range of customers. A holistic approach is required for developing strong channels across the board. Some of the smart bankers I know are taking the money they save through branch transformation and using it to fund more innovative mobile and online initiatives. As Danny suggests, you have to look at all of your channels and figure out the right mix of investments. You want to make sure that each channel gets the attention it deserves, and that you're not robbing Peter to pay Paul.

Develop a Customer Strategy

Keeping customers happy should be a major goal of your mobile channel initiatives. For many industries, the idea that happy customers are important to the success of a business venture is accepted as gospel truth.

In banking, however, the concept of customer-centricity is still relatively new. Most banks are still structured as product-centric organizations. In other words, almost all of their activities and operations revolve around their products. For most banks, the customer is incidental to the process.

The idea of customer lifetime value is well known to most banks, but still not hardwired into the mentality of most bank executives. Most retailers have aggressively embraced the wisdom of putting the customer at the center of their business strategies. You don't have to convince them—they already get it, and all they think about is keeping the customer happy.

That is not the case with banks—at least not yet. As the speed of business continues accelerating, and as more financial transactions move to mobile devices, it will be increasingly difficult to hide the genuine apathy and deep indifference that many bankers exhibit when dealing with their customers.

As a result, the biggest challenge of mobile banking won't be technological—it will be cultural. Banks will have to overcome their age-old instinct to treat customers poorly. In place of that instinct, banks will need carefully planned and well-executed strategies for satisfying and delighting customers at every touch point and through each channel.

Here's what banks really need to understand: Mobile strips away the friction, opacity, and mystery that has characterized their relationships with customers for centuries. When your customers have a mobile device, you have nowhere to hide.

Are you ready for mobile-empowered customers? Do you have 360-degree views of your customers? Can you calculate their lifetime value, across all of your product lines? Do you understand their social habits so you can market effectively to them and to their friends? Can you track their buying behaviors so you can integrate your efforts more closely with external partners such as retailers, service providers, and credit card companies? Are you using big data and predictive analytics to make better decisions about launching new products and opening new markets?

Open Up Your App Store

Although our mobile devices certainly possess many intrinsic capabilities, what we really value about them are the apps. Without the apps, they're just fancy telephones and sleek tablets.

Keep that thought in mind, because it also applies to the world of mobile banking. Apps enable customers to perform mobile banking operations on their mobile devices. Without specialized apps, there is no mobile banking.

If you're a banker, you need to ask yourself, "Where do I get apps and how do I get those apps onto the mobile devices of my customers?"

Not too long ago, the answer would have been: "Draw up a detailed list of specifications and give it to the chief information officer (CIO) because the CIO already has app developers in the IT department, and if you ask nicely, they might put it on their list of future deliverables."

At some banks, that might still be the way it's done. Increasingly, however, banks are creating public web application programming interfaces (APIs) that essentially enable developers anywhere to create apps for them. Gartner predicts that by 2016, half of the world's leading banks will have a platform for public web APIs.

Admittedly, many banks will struggle with the idea of open or public web APIs. But the advantages will quickly overwhelm the naysayers. Public APIs rapidly accelerate the app development process by encouraging and enabling collaboration. Instead of just relying on the handful or developers in your IT shop, open APIs literally open the development process up to the entire world. Any developer—or any customer with programming abilities—who has something to contribute is free to pitch in and lend a hand.

As Gartner notes, API platforms enable third-party developers to build highly customized apps for very specific needs.

67

Let's say you have a small but highly profitable group of mobile customers with a specific need or demand. The customers in that particular group can be highly influential and you want to keep them happy. In the past it would have required spending millions of dollars and taken a team of developers several years to create a specialized piece of software. Today, that software can be effectively sourced to a global population of developers and completed in weeks, at a reasonable cost.

With open APIs, you can innovate at Internet speed. They give you an incredible advantage over competitors who insist on developing their software the old-fashioned way. When an app is finished, you put it in your app store and, voilà, your customers can download it onto their mobile devices and begin using it immediately.

Open APIs, public development platforms, and app stores are fundamental parts of the emerging mobile app ecosystem. The more you know about how app development works, the better prepared you will be for your discussions with your CIO and other IT people you will need to sustain your mobile banking project.

I recently discovered an excellent post, "2014: Year of the Open Ecosystem," written by Greg Satell for his blog, *Digital Tonto*. Here is a brief excerpt from his post that is especially relevant to the topic we're discussing:

> *When Steve Jobs and Apple launched the iPhone in June of 2007, it was an instant hit. Hundreds of consumers lined up at stores to be among the first to buy one and millions were sold in the first year. After only five quarters it surpassed BlackBerry—the market leader at the time—and became a consumer icon.*
>
> *Yet it wasn't till a year later that Apple really changed the world. That was when the app store arrived. 10 million apps were downloaded in the first three days and that number*

grew into more than a billion within a year. Looking back at those early apps, they seem amazingly primitive, but at the time they were revolutionary.

Apple, in essence, transformed the iPhone from a consumer product to an ecosystem. The company provided tools like software development kits (SDKs) and application programming interfaces (APIs) so that anyone, anywhere could alter and improve the functionality of Apple products.

It also created a major advantage for Apple. Anyone who wanted to compete with it would have to not only match its capabilities and performance, but the collective efforts of thousands of independent developers, all striving to create something useful for Apple's legions of fans.

And it's not just Apple anymore. Today, brands are becoming platforms that rely less on the features of their products and more on the breadth and quality of their connections.[2]

I truly believe that Greg's post hits the nail on the head. It really makes us think about the role that modern brands play in our rapidly evolving digitally connected global economy.

Banks Aren't Your Only Competitors

Jim Tosone is an experienced IT executive, and he keeps a close eye on the software developer community. I asked him recently to share his perspective on mobile app development for banking, and I want to share his valuable insights with you. First, Jim notes that when we talk about competition in mobile banking, we tend to think mostly about retail banks; we forget that many players in the mobile banking space aren't traditional retail banks. American Express and USAA, for example, aren't retail banks in the strictest sense. But if you compete in the mobile banking space, you have to stay aware of what they're doing.

At our request, Jim prepared a list of key elements required for effective mobile banking apps. We should add that Jim, the creator of the Improvisation Means Business program, is a strong proponent of agile software development methodology. So don't be surprised that his recommendations track closely with agile practices and techniques.

"The key elements of agility are simplicity, pragmatism, iteration, adaptive planning, rapid response, adaptability," says Jim. "When you look at mobile banking apps from a developer's perspective, you see those actual elements in varying degrees. For instance, City Bank Texas has an app that allows customers to view their balances and reward status without logging in. That would be an example of simplicity. Capital One has an app that allows customers to 'bump' [transfer] money between phones. That's an example of pragmatism. BBVA Compass Bank has already released multiple generations of iPad apps. That's an example of iteration."

I really appreciate the sense of detail and granularity that Jim brings to the conversation. I should mention that he was a longtime IT leader at Pfizer, so he definitely understands the importance of fine details. Jim also raises another matter that I hadn't previously considered: As mobile banking apps become more commonly accepted and are used more widely, customers will expect branch personnel to offer help when they have problems with their apps or need some kind of technical support. That means that people who work in branches will have to be trained—even if the training is only rudimentary—to offer some level of basic tech support to customers with questions about their mobile banking apps. I'm not saying that every branch needs a help desk, but it seems fairly clear that customers will ask technical questions and will expect reasonably helpful answers.

"Since updates will occur more frequently with mobile apps than with online apps, the people working in the branches will have to become more agile themselves to keep up with the most current version of their bank's apps," says Jim. "This also applies to the people working in the bank's call centers. They're probably accustomed to keeping up with changes in the bank's online software, but now they have to keep up with changes in the bank's mobile apps, which will be updated on a more rapid timetable."

Jim's insight, which is based on his experience, is absolutely priceless. In many ways, banks will have to start thinking more like IT organizations and develop the capabilities required to deal with ongoing technical support issues.

"Creating an agile mind-set is critical because things will be constantly changing," says Jim. In a very real sense, mobility is forcing banks to cope with a cultural shift. In the past, change generally happened only when something was broken. Today, change is considered an opportunity to be embraced, not a problem to be solved. Smart organizations will figure out ways to make people comfortable with change. When people accept change as natural, there are fewer disconnects between their expectations and the realities of the environment.

Today, change is the one unalterable reality of almost every competitive situation. Business organizations that don't learn to love change will lose market share to their more nimble competitors.

API-ifying Your Bank

While I don't want to turn this book into a technical discourse, certain aspects of software development are incredibly relevant to our worldview as bankers. The idea that modern banks—or any modern business, for that matter—can rely on traditional software development methodologies for creating software for consumer markets is ludicrous. That kind of thinking just won't fly in today's rapidly changing world. You might as well be driving a Stanley Steamer in the Indianapolis 500.

Increasingly, software is developed by groups of outside developers working through APIs. Here's a beautiful observation from Robin Vasan, managing director at the Mayfield Fund:

> *Developers now expect the same instant gratification as end users. Instead of having to download, configure and manage all the associated software components, more and more of these capabilities need to be packaged "as-a-service"—hence, the move to cloud services. It is also important to remember that software development is an art, and programmers want a very simple and elegant programming interface.*
>
> *. . . it seems that the promise of service oriented architectures is finally being realized, and it is creating a strong opportunity for innovative business models.*[3]

From Robin's perspective, the world is "API-ifying," and woe to companies that don't understand—or outright resist—that trend. As Robin correctly notes, "Facebook has hundreds of APIs across such social areas as friends, photos, likes, and events. Google has thousands of APIs across search/AdWords, web analytics, YouTube, maps, e-mail, and many more. Amazon has APIs that cover the spectrum from Alexa web traffic rankings to e-commerce product and pricing information and even the ability to start and stop individual machines."

APIs are the future, and smart companies are getting on the bandwagon. The API-ification of business extends beyond consumer-facing apps—it also includes business process software that consumers never see. In a very real sense, API-ification represents a triumph for the concept of service-oriented architecture

(SOA), which enables the creation of new software from pieces or modules of existing software—sort of a LEGO model for software development.

Remind Me, Why Are We Doing This?

I would like to end this chapter by slightly reframing the overall value proposition of mobile banking. Up until this point, I have been suggesting that mobile banking is valuable mostly because it enables traditional banks to extend existing lines of business into new markets and fight off encroachments by nontraditional rivals such as retailers and telecoms. In a sense, my argument has been focused on finding value outside the organization.

Now I will add another pillar to support my argument by suggesting that mobile banking can serve as a platform or rallying point for the creation of new and dramatic efficiencies within the business itself. In other words, mobile banking offers internal as well as external benefits. Moreover, the internal benefits might prove as valuable, or possibly even more valuable, than the external benefits, particularly when viewed from a long-term perspective.

In June 2013, Torsten Eistert and Mathias Ullrich of the consulting firm A.T. Kearney produced an excellent paper, "Reducing Complexity in Retail Banking: Simple Wins Every Time," in which they argue persuasively that most banks should streamline and simplify their product portfolios. Here is a great passage from the paper:

> *Like houses with attics full of worn-out armchairs and discarded tables hidden above newly decorated living rooms, most banks have a stockpile of overhauled, outdated products tucked away behind a few shiny innovations. Many of*

these products require complex activities but have nothing to do with new sales. And the glut of products is limiting not only profits but also the flexibility to react to external pressures.[4]

Eistert and Ullrich recommend cleaning out "the attic," and point out that portfolio clutter isn't just messy; it also reduces profitability. Here is another excerpt from their paper:

Consider the front office: More products means bank tellers need extra time to explain and process transactions for a variety of products, features, prices, and discounts. Each transaction is likely to have a whole new set of relevant products for tellers to juggle, from cash payments and making deposits to selling investment funds and saving plans and even educating customers about new interest rates for certificates of deposit. This highly complex front office not only frustrates customers who expect flawless treatment; it also drives cost-to-serve up significantly. . . .

Even new sales can cut into profits. When customers can't clearly see why some products cost more than others, sales advisors often offer discounts as a last resort to meet their demands. These discounts are usually tied to a trial period, but converting trial period prices back to standard prices does not always happen for fear of losing customers.

The authors also note that overly complex product portfolios can keep IT cost unnecessarily high, writing that "It is not uncommon for banks to keep certain legacy systems running because they host a large portfolio of legacy loans or long-term mortgages and prefer not to have to contact clients in the event of system migration problems." Does this sound like a description of your bank? I know lots of bankers who would nod readily in agreement!

Eistert and Ullrich point to three reasons for portfolio clutter:

1. A product-centric rather than customer-centric view of the world
2. Absence of clear rules and processes for monitoring product life cycles and terminating obsolete or unprofitable products
3. Overly complex product blueprints due to hundreds of product variations, multiple brands, and accumulated legacy products

The authors recommend building bank products the way that automobile manufacturers like Toyota build cars, using a modular approach that incorporates lean manufacturing principles. Instead of offering thousands of different products to harried customers—essentially you're forcing them to spend hours trying to decipher the differences between similar products—doesn't it make more sense to offer a streamlined portfolio of basic products that can be easily customized or tailored to meet specific customer needs?

I believe that mobile banking can act as the catalyst, the platform, and the process for the kind of ongoing portfolio simplification that Eistert and Ullrich call for in their paper. Why not reverse engineer the portfolio, working backward from the apps that people want on their mobile devices? Seriously, if they don't want the app, they don't want the service behind it. It will be easy enough to tell which apps are popular by checking the metrics generated by your app store. If no one is downloading a particular app, don't merely kill the app—kill the service behind it, too!

Maybe instead of thinking like traditional bankers, we should be thinking more like gardeners. Every gardener knows the key to successful gardening is constant vigilance and daily care. You need to pull the weeds before they overwhelm the plants you are trying to grow. That's our problem today—too many weeds and not enough gardeners.

Notes

1. http://jimmarous.blogspot.com/
2. www.digitaltonto.com/2014/2014-year-of-the-open-ecosystem/?utm_source=Digital%20Tonto%20Newsletter&utm_campaign=64d2c0bb01-2014_The_Year_Of_The_Open_Ecosystem1_5_2014&utm_medium=email&utm_term=0_3e316dce-2-64d2c0bb01-389202633
3. http://gigaom.com/2012/05/28/the-api-ificiation-of-software-and-legos/
4. www.atkearney.com/financial-institutions/featured-article/-/asset_publisher/j8IucAqMqEhB/content/reducing-complexity-in-retail-banking-simple-wins-every-time/10192

CHAPTER 6

Prepaid Cards

A Step in the Right Direction

I believe in the benevolent power of banking. I believe that banking is good for humankind and that when banks are managed properly, they serve the very real needs of individuals, families, communities, and nations. Most of what you read in this book is an argument in favor of banking. Historically and traditionally, banking is foundational to the slow but sure creation and distribution of wealth across our increasingly connected global economy.

I'm not delusional. I understand that wealth is not shared evenly or fairly. But I am what author Matt Ridley would describe as a "rational optimist."

Banks help people store, save, and spend their money. Without banks, those of us with money would have to hide it under our mattresses or bring it with us whenever we wanted to make a purchase, and those of us without money would be forced to depend on loan sharks and other predatory lenders whenever we needed cash, whether to pay the grocer, the plumber, or the pediatrician.

I am for anything that affords more people the opportunity to use banks. For many people, the mobile telephone will offer a path to banking. Prepaid cards offer another path.

We drive cars because of Henry Ford, not Karl Benz. We use personal computers because of Bill Gates, not Steve Jobs. That is, until the Mac came on the scene (that said the PC still has a lot of loyal followers (the author uses both). We use smartphones because of Steve Jobs, not Mike Lazaridis (the inventor of the BlackBerry). In many cases, good enough is just fine. The solution doesn't have to be perfect; it just has to be effective, practical, and affordable.

The prepaid card is a great example of a solution that isn't ideal, but is good enough for now. In this chapter, we look at how prepaid cards work and examine some of the opportunities they present.

But first, some background. In the United States, as many as 52 million people are considered unbanked or underbanked. In today's competitive environment, that's too big a market for banks to ignore. For the past two or three years, banks have been fighting for a share of the unbanked/underbanked market. One of the primary weapons in that fight is the prepaid card.

Another powerful force driving the adoption of prepaid cards by banks is something more primitive: the urge to survive. Banks were caught off guard by upstarts like PayPal, which now transacts trillions of dollars of payments. Ten years ago, all of those transactions would have been handled by banks. Now, banks are struggling to recover what they perceive as lost ground. Banks are also scrambling to hang on to territory that is threatened by an even newer generation of companies that are hoping to duplicate PayPal's success.

It's easy to see why banks see prepaid cards as a great opportunity. The prepaid card market is experiencing double-digit, year-over-year growth in multiple markets in numerous countries, including the United States, Brazil, Mexico, Italy, India, Canada, Russia, and parts of the Middle East. Worldwide, total loadable volume is expected to reach nearly $1 trillion.

Here are some useful data points:[1]

- The open-loop prepaid card market is growing across countries and is expected to reach $822 billion of gross dollar volume (GDV) by 2017 at a compound annual growth rate (CAGR) of 22 percent from 2010. (Open-loop cards are typically general purpose cards that are issued by banks and most likely carry an Amex, Visa, Mastercard, or Discover logo and can be used in places where they are accepted. Acceptance is confirmed by the merchant. They are also typically likely to have a fee component. Closed-loop cards can be used only in a single store or group of stores much like Starbucks Cards or Best Buy cards.)
- Total dollar volume loaded on the closed-loop prepaid card is estimated to be $243.6 billion in 2012. Growth of the closed-loop prepaid card market is relatively stagnant and is expected to remain the same in the near future.
- In addition to the United States, several other countries, including Brazil, Mexico, Italy, United Kingdom/Ireland, India, Canada, Russia, and Saudi Arabia/United Arab Emirates, are expected to play a key role in driving the growth of prepaid through 2017, and they are expected to contribute a cumulative 31 percent of the open-loop prepaid card market.

Banks see prepaid cardholders as natural potential customers. Banks already issue plenty of plastic cards, and prepaid cards are perceived as a logical addition to the existing portfolio of retail banking products.

Another reason that banks find prepaid cards attractive is that the U.S. government already uses them to distribute benefits to millions of recipients, every day, in every state of the union.

If you are a bank, the government is already one of your most important customers. In addition to being a large customer, the government buys many different kinds of banking services, everything from checking accounts to pension management. No bank wants to lose government business, and the idea of losing shares of the prepaid card market to nonbanking organizations is anathema to traditional bankers.

When I worked at Citibank, most government benefits were distributed by sending checks through the mail. This was an inefficient method for two reasons: (1) It was expensive to prepare and mail the checks, and (2) after you put the check in the mail, it was difficult to ascertain if the intended recipient had actually received the payment. If a check wasn't cashed, we had no way of knowing if the cause was a bad address, an honest mistake by a letter carrier, theft, confusion (a lot of benefit recipients are elderly or infirm), or one of a hundred other possible reasons.

We mailed millions of checks on behalf of the government, and we hoped that most of them reached the right person. As you can imagine, fraud was a problem. Sometimes a recipient died and his or her relatives kept cashing the checks. We really had no way of knowing.

Interestingly, this hasn't been a problem for government just in the United States. In Europe, governments distribute pension benefits to retirees who have relocated to various parts of the world. Some of those retirees now live in the United States, and European agencies have found themselves dealing with many of the same issues that have faced the U.S. government and its multitudes of agencies.

Today, most government benefits are distributed electronically, via direct deposit into checking accounts. But a large portion is paid directly onto prepaid cards, which makes the government a major player in the prepaid card market.

For the government, the main advantages of prepaid cards are lower operational costs and reduced waste. Using prepaid cards to distribute benefits also generates enormous amounts of data that can be analyzed and converted into useful insights, which can drive greater efficiencies down the road. Prepaid cards also give the government more control, because now it can say, "Here is your card; don't lose it. If you lose it, your benefits will be delayed."

Generally speaking, however, prepaid cards have the potential to move funds into circulation much faster than checks. The greater speed of digital banking, in all of its many forms, creates a ripple effect through the entire benefits system and impacts all of its stakeholders, including the millions of small businesses serving the people and families receiving benefits. Let's be honest: When you need cash, you need it fast. So speed is good.

Big banks like Citi and JPMorgan Chase want to play aggressively in the prepaid card space, but their cost structures can make it difficult for them to compete with newer nonbank companies such as NetSpend, Green Dot, AccountNow, and MoneyGram, which operate at significantly lower costs and are able to generate higher margins on prepaid transactions than the big banks.

Nonbanks are able to operate at lower costs for a couple of reasons. Some of the nonbanks have developed their own networks. Some have developed their own processing technologies. As a result of their previous investments in technology and infrastructure, they now enjoy competitive advantages and don't have to rely on third-party vendors to operate. That means they can operate at much lower costs than most traditional banks.

Because they are newer, the nonbanks have been able to choose their locations more economically, picking relatively low-cost states for their operating centers. Another advantage they enjoy is less regulation. Nonbanks aren't regulated as tightly as traditional banks, so compliance is less of a cost factor than it is for established banks.

Legacy systems are also a problem for established banks that want to compete in the prepaid space. The information technology (IT) systems of a large bank are very tightly integrated. From a business perspective, tight integration of enterprise IT systems is a net positive. But the same integration that makes it easier to operate an enterprise-wide IT system efficiently makes it very difficult to introduce innovations quickly, since changes to one part of the system cannot be done without impacting other parts of the system. As a result, innovation has become a real challenge for large banks.

Yet another hurdle is outsourcing. Many large banks have outsourced large portions of their operations to companies such as IBM, Accenture, and other global providers. Those outsourcing arrangements are often complex, and they are difficult to change in midstream. Thus outsourcing itself tends to be an impediment to innovation, at least for the larger banks.

Another item: The processing fees charged by traditional banks are limited by law. As mentioned earlier, nonbanks are not as tightly regulated as traditional banks. As a consequence, nonbanks have more leeway when it comes to charging fees.

Last but not least, the nonbanks tend to see themselves as start-ups, and often operate with a start-up mentality. They tend to be more flexible, more nimble, and less risk-averse than traditional banks. All of those qualities give them an advantage over traditional banks in new or emerging markets, where it's more difficult to predict what will happen and there isn't a track record of success to provide guidance.

In summary, there are numerous economic incentives for banks to compete in the prepaid card market, and many hurdles for them to overcome. Not surprisingly, we are beginning to see nonbanks acquiring existing banks, and it won't be long before traditional banks begin acquiring nonbanks. It's not clear how the new hybrid entities will operate, but it certainly indicates that the industry is evolving very quickly. I also know for a fact that the traditional banks and the new players see the prepaid card phenomenon as a stepping-stone to a more comprehensive mobile payment system. It's not hard to envision the evolutionary path from checks to wire to prepaid to mobile. It's only a matter of when and how fast it happens.

Financial Inclusion

Let's step back for a moment and ask ourselves why the prepaid card phenomenon is important. My short answer is that prepaid cards are a significant step on the path toward financial inclusion for the 2.5 billon people worldwide who need financial services but cannot get them. Imagine the boost the global economy would receive if 2.5 billion people suddenly had access to safe, legal, and regulated financial services on a daily basis.

The goal of worldwide financial inclusion isn't a pipedream or a banker's fantasy. It is real, it is achievable, and it is necessary if we want the global economy to keep growing at a healthy pace. I see the unbanked and the underbanked as potential customers. Our goal should be getting them into the financial system as quickly as possible.

Obviously, prepaid cards are a step in the right direction. But getting prepaid cards into the hands of 2.5 billion people isn't a job for a handful of organizations or a single industry. It's going to take a full-on partnership between government and the private sector to make it happen.

As suggested earlier, government and private industry have already formed partnerships to serve the prepaid card market. The next task is putting some formal structure around the existing framework, creating a truly robust system, and scaling it up to global proportions.

The other positive aspect of a prepaid card is that is serves as a kind of pre–credit card. What do I mean by that? Simply that a prepaid card provides utility that is very similar to that of a credit card, at a lower cost than a credit card. Think of it this way: Both credit cards and prepaid cards eliminate the need for cash and remove friction from transactions. Both tend to raise levels of safety and security. Both create an audit trail that can be monitored and analyzed.

From the bank's perspective, one advantage of a prepaid card is that it doesn't require a credit check, which immediately lowers the bank's cost. Another advantage of the prepaid card is that the bank is not required to hold a reserve, which frees up its working capital. In the case of credit cards, the bank is required to hold a reserve to safeguard against the possibly of default by the cardholder.

Theoretically, at least, the fees charged for a prepaid card should be lower than the fees charged for a credit card (fees charged by a prepaid card are lower as there is no credit risk as it is prefunded. Because it is prefunded, a bank does not have to set apart capital as it is not a credit product), which works to the consumer's advantage. The other advantage for the consumer is that a prepaid card, because it can be tracked, can help the cardholder build up a financial history, which can be very useful when he or she applies for credit at some point in the future.

The Present and Future of Prepaid

The upside of prepaid is huge. Prepaid cards have the potential to serve 2.5 billion adults worldwide who currently have no relationship with a bank. This untapped market isn't restricted to Asia, Africa, and the Middle East. It covers a wide swath of the globe. Anyone who doesn't have access to the existing banking infrastructure is a potential customer. That includes:

- People who are paid in cash and don't have bank accounts
- People who are paid by check and don't have bank accounts

- People who pay their bills in cash because they don't have checking accounts
- People who cannot afford to pay the fees charged by traditional banks
- People who rely on predatory lenders when they are short of cash

Drivers of change in the prepaid market include:

- *Renewed focus on financial inclusion.* Corporations are also serving financial inclusion either due to government compulsion or motivated by sound business judgment, by converting cash and checks to electronic payouts for their underbanked employees. The corporate payroll opportunity is projected to reach $191 billion globally by 2017.
- *Cost-effective option for organizations.* Prepaid cards enable both commercial and government entities to increase financial inclusion while reducing processing costs and increasing efficiency and risk management.
- *Growing acceptance of general purpose reloadable (GPR) cards.* The increasing availability of GPR cards at retail point of sale (POS) is also driving the migration of cash to electronic payments.
- *No capital required for prepaid operation.* Unlike credit cards, where banks are required to keep a certain amount of capital to start credit card operations, prepaid card business can be easily started without any major capital investment.

There has also been significant movement on the regulatory front. In the United States, the Durbin Amendment to the Dodd-Frank Act has carved out interchange fees for prepaid cards. As per the Durbin Amendment implemented on October 1, 2011, the Federal Reserve ruled that debit interchange fees would be capped at 21 cents plus 0.05 percent of the transaction.

The prepaid card industry is largely spared from this amendment, as the closed-loop reloadable prepaid cards are exempted from interchange fees while the open-loop, network-branded, and nonreloadable cards will be subject to interchange fees.

At present, the market for the open-loop cards is relatively small compared to the closed-loop market. Closed-loop prepaid cards can only be used for issuers' products or for limited purposes such as prepaid gift cards, whereas open-loop cards can be utilized for multiple purposes, such as making purchases at various stores or paying bills.

Changes in the regulation of overdraft fees are also having an impact. On August 22, 2010, the Federal Reserve introduced Regulation E, which limits the overdraft fees that can be charged to accounts. In addition to this, customers have to opt in if they want overdraft protection. (The impact of overdraft fees on prepaid cards is minimal, as most prepaid cards do not provide overdraft protection and the funds have to be deposited prior to use.) Loss of overdraft fees has led to banks look for alternative sources of revenues, including prepaid cards.

As a result of the regulatory changes, banks are raising fees on basic accounts, and at the same time are offering prepaid cards to customers who are leaving the bank because of the higher fees.

Banks like the prepaid cards because they aren't subject to the same restrictions under the U.S. Dodd-Frank Act that shrank the revenue collected from merchants on debit card purchases. The prepaid cards also don't carry any credit risk for the banks because cardholders are using their own money.

Business Takes Prepaid Seriously

Some companies aren't waiting for the banks to figure out the prepaid market. Wal-Mart Stores and American Express have partnered to launch Bluebird, a new prepaid debit card.

The Bluebird card doesn't have a monthly maintenance fee, annual fee, or activation fee. (Prepaid cards offered by banks carry fees of $5 or more a month, in addition to activation fees and charges for talking to a customer service representative, checking balances at automated teller machines, and other activities.)

Wal-Mart and American Express looked at the numbers and decided to move ahead on their own. The combined number of prepaid debit and payroll card users is expected to reach 12.4 million in the United States by 2014. That's a huge potential market, and neither Wal-Mart nor American Express wants to be left behind. They watched as nonbank companies like Green Dot and NetSpend made inroads in the financial services market. They also saw that drastic reductions in the number of traditional debit card transactions were strengthening the case for prepaid debit cards.

Make no mistake—the banks are paying close attention to the prepaid market, as shown in Figure 6.1. It strikes me as more interesting, however, when nonbank actors jump onto the stage and strike gold in previously undiscovered markets.

College students, for example, represent a largely underserved market. Only 11 percent of students arriving at college have a checking account. Enterprising companies like HigherOne have found a great opportunity in that market, offering students so-called refund cards that issue refunds from their colleges. (Refunds would be issued when there are instances of overcharging a student for a term, or if a grant is offered retroactively or the fee structure reduces after the admission process is complete. In some cases, a student is issued a reimbursement for completing certain requirements, such as becoming certified in a particular skill.) If you don't at present have a child in college or know someone in college, it probably doesn't sound like a big deal. But refunds add up quickly, and HigherOne devised a system for loading the refunds onto

TABLE 6.1 Recent Examples of Consolidation in the Prepaid Cards Industry

Activity	Category	Description	Rationale
U.S. Bank	Vertical consolidation	U.S. Bank is acquiring FSV Payments Systems, a prepaid card processor. The deal is expected to be completed soon.	The acquisition is expected to strengthen U.S. Bank's position in the prepaid market. The prepaid market has been its strategic focus over the past decade, and the acquisition will help it offer a full suite of prepaid services.
Wal-Mart and American Express	Strategic alliance	In October 2012, Wal-Mart and American Express launched a new prepaid debit card called Bluebird.	The move is intended to strengthen both companies' positions in the prepaid card market.
JPMorgan Chase's GPR prepaid card	Entry by banks in prepaid card space	In July 2012, Chase launched its own general purpose reloadable (GPR) prepaid card branded Chase Liquid.	JPMorgan Chase entered into the prepaid market to become a part of the growing prepaid card business and to recover fee revenue losses due to various financial regulations.
Fifth Third Bank's reloadable prepaid card launch	Entry by banks in prepaid card space	In November 2012, Fifth Third Bank (5/3 Bank), a U.S.-based regional bank, launched a reloadable prepaid card, Access 360.	The bank expects additional revenue from the prepaid card line of business.

prepaid cards. The system is currently used by 1.2 million college students.

Banks are also stumbling into the area of so-called second-chance accounts. Most banks have nothing to offer customers who are not deemed eligible for a checking account. Again, from my perspective, that's letting money walk out the door. Prepaid cards enable banks to establish relationships with customers who aren't eligible for a checking account today, but who might become eligible tomorrow. In this area, I fault the banks for ignoring the potential lifetime value of an individual customer, which can be nurtured and grown over time.

ATMs and Prepaid Cards

My good friend Todd Nuttall is a former vice president and chief financial officer at American Express Worldwide Technology Finance, where he oversaw all spending on data centers and data operations worldwide. Earlier in his career, he worked at Boeing during the creation of the Boeing 777 aircraft program. Today, he is the CEO of Better ATM Services, a technology innovation company linking the ATM and prepaid industries.

"We've developed a simple set of technologies that allows today's existing ATMs to dispense prepaid cards such as Visa and MasterCard directly from the ATM cash tray," says Todd. "We're helping banks to bridge an important gap in the service they provide to their customers."

From Todd's perspective, it makes little sense for banks to cede the prepaid market to nonbank players. "People who use ATMs also buy prepaid cards, but they buy those cards at other locations," says Todd. "Why not keep that business at the bank?"

Interview with Todd Nuttall

I recently asked Todd to respond to a series of questions about the future of banking, and his replies were so informative that I decided to include them in the book verbatim, with minimal editing.

S.K.: Generally, how is technology changing the relationships between banks and their customers?

T.N.: Technology is changing *everything* about relationships between banks and their customers. For most people, banking meant writing checks, balancing checkbooks, and visiting the branch frequently for deposits, withdrawals, and other very basic services. Today, online bill payment and the ease of debit card transactions have practically eliminated the need for checks. Online banking services have reduced the need to send out monthly statements since bank customers can quickly check their transactions online, or automatically transfer information to products such as Quicken or MS Money. Now with cell phone applications, we see mobile banking fulfill the need of tracking balances, verifying transactions, alerting to issues, and even check cashing. I just cashed a check using my phone two hours ago!

An important change involves the continuing expansion and improvement of ATM technology. ATMs now can handle cash and check deposits immediately, without envelopes and without delays in posting transactions. But it's much more than that. With all of the above, the need to actually visit a bank branch has been diminished dramatically. Based on my own personal experience, I estimate that the need to visit a branch has been reduced by 80 percent. The result is that banks are realizing that it is important to leverage the time-and-place benefits of ATMs giving customers what they want, where they want it. Banks are shrinking their footprints in favor of ATM microcenters where multifunctional ATMs are the customer interface.

As a result, banks must establish entirely new relationships with their customers in this new branchless business environment. I don't think we have yet seen a real winner or break-through in this area. In fact, what we've seen is the growth of services like Amex Bluebird, which essentially replaces the need for traditional bank branches. In effect, banks are being disintermediated by companies using technology to offer banklike services.

S.K.: From your perspective, what does an ideal customer experience look like?

T.N.: I like when my chosen organization actually *does* something for me. That said, it's hard to describe "ideal," since every person is very different and we are pleased by different tastes, colors, and interaction.

In my case, I'm a control freak but I hate to waste my time in basic data work. For example, I use Quicken to manage my finances but have found it woefully inadequate. The Quicken interface is ancient-looking, and it requires a lot of technical skill to link all my accounts and credit cards.

The ideal customer experience is a single source that tracks, records, and categorizes *all* of my financial needs. People use the payment or financial method they find most appropriate or most convenient for the task at hand. Credit cards, debit cards, and prepaid cards have not entirely replaced cash; they simply slipped in to fill a need.

Rarely do payment methodologies disappear or get completely replaced. It's still common for individuals to use all of the available payment methods—cash and coin for some things, checks for a few things, online bill payment for some payments and transfers, PayPal and similar systems for some things, debit cards for some things and credit cards for others, and even prepaid cards for budgeting or giving money to kids as allowances.

I see mobile payments growing, but not replacing the existing payment methodologies. People will use the payment method most convenient to the situation.

In addition to managing all kinds of payment methods, the ideal customer experience would include all the necessary tracking on the back end, so essentially it would appear as though all of my payments were made from a single financial platform. So the ideal experience would also include collecting receipts and purchase transaction information electronically, and then filing it or linking it to my individual transactions. Think of how much that would help when you're filing tax returns.

S.K.: What are the barriers and challenges that modern bankers must overcome?

T.N.: History! Banks have hundreds of years of being *the institution*. Much of this is for good reasons—controls, safety, accuracy, and so on. However, the same features that make the banks safe also make them slow to innovate. I have yet to see a bank that truly seeks innovation at the bleeding edge.

That's why we've seen many of new entrants into the traditional financial services channels. For example, new billion-dollar entities like Green Dot, NetSpend, PayPal, and others would never have gotten started if banks had actively sought to fill these needs.

These new companies thrive on innovation and will likely serve as complete replacements to traditional banking within a few years. The bank as we have known it may not need to exist! Some of these companies launch a new product or feature every six weeks. I've never seen a bank move at that speed.

S.K.: What are the best ways for bankers to lock in customer loyalty?

T.N.:The strategy they use today is making it hard to close your account and shift to another institution. Several times I have been so fed up with my bank I would have moved if it had been easier. But by the time you could open new accounts, balance out all the outstanding transactions, and replace all the services and logins, PINs, and cards, you will have invested many hours or days to make the change. Banks have relied on this as their strategy for ensuring loyalty, but it's very shortsighted and will work against them in the long run.

One day, perhaps soon, a bank that is hungry for new customers will offer some kind of irresistible incentive and then have specially trained staff at the ready to help new customers transition easily from their current banks to the new bank. That would lower the barriers that make it hard to switch banks and would build good relationships with new customers at the same time.

Ultimately, though, banks have to prove that they are looking out for you and that they care about you. For example, my company is building the capability to link a customer's ATM-issued gift cards so if for some reason the balance isn't used before the expiration date, the money is automatically returned to the customer's account. That kind of service builds trust and customer loyalty by putting the customer's needs front and center.

S.K.: Many banking services are now offered by nonbank companies such as retailers and telecoms. How will traditional retail banks deal with the influx of competition?

T.N.: Great question. I believe that banks are in for a wake-up call. Micropayments can add up to big numbers. Telecoms have understood that for a long time. For decades they've been collecting a few cents here and a few cents there on short phone calls. It adds up to billions in revenue. But until recently, you really couldn't use a traditional payment card for purchases under $10.

Banks are still learning how to thrive in the micropayments world. Meanwhile, the retailers aren't wasting time. I've heard that nearly 25 percent of all of Target sales are paid for with Target prepaid products! This entirely bypasses Visa/MasterCard and traditional banking transactions.

I also asked Todd where he sees the retail banking industry heading in the next five to 10 years. Here's his list of predictions:

- Dramatic increase in off-branch services offered at ATMs and kiosks
- Linkages to national and local consumer brands that provide valuable services and products to specific customers
- Greater alignment to particular customer segments (women, artists, techies, vegans, etc.)
- Destruction of banks that cannot compete successfully against newcomers and emerging specialty products

"There is still a lot of pressure building under the surface," says Todd. "The catch-22 is that focusing on today's problems will not prepare you for dealing with tomorrow's problems. It takes great leadership to manage the present and anticipate the future."

For Todd, the ideal leader is someone like Alan Mullaly, the CEO at Ford Motor Company. He explained why: "I had the great fortune of being mentored by Alan early in my career when we were at Boeing. As CEO at Ford, he saw the looming danger and restructured the company to survive financial hard times and create ultramodern vehicles that people would buy. Ford was the only major U.S. automaker that did not require a federal bailout, and it now sets the standard for innovation in the automotive industry. It's very hard to find leaders like Alan, but that is what we need in the banking industry."

Building Trust with Customers

Most of the discussion around mobile banking tends to focus on issues of technology and economics. Don Peppers, the dean of one-to-one marketing and customer relationship management, says the real challenge facing players in the mobile banking space is establishing and sustaining "trustability."

First a bit of background on Don: Back in the early 1990s, he and Martha Rogers wrote *The One to One Future*, a best seller that made the case for customer-centric marketing strategies. Today, customer-centricity might seem like a no-brainer, but until Don and Martha wrote their book, most companies were perfectly happy to stick with the product-centric strategies that had sustained them during the decades that stretched from the end of World War II in 1945 to the disintegration the Soviet Union in 1991.

Don and Martha followed the success of their first book with a series of one-to-one marketing books. They became popular speakers and launched a boutique consultancy, the Peppers and Rogers Group. Their latest book is *Extreme Trust: Honesty as a Competitive Advantage.*[2] In the book, they criticize retail banks for relying on fees to generate a large portion of their revenues. The fees, they contend, radically undermine trust between the banks and their customers. In a telephone interview with us in late 2013, Don warned that retail banks can no longer rely primarily on trust to compete successfully against nonbank firms in the mobile banking space.

"I would not say that retail banks have the advantage when it comes to trust," says Don. "Banks have a business model that is designed primarily to increase the fees they can charge a customer. It's no secret that debit cards tend to increase the number of overdraft fees incurred by consumers. Those fees have done a lot to destroy the trust of banking customers over the past 20 years."

Consumers trust retail banks to "keep their money safe and return it to them when they ask for it," says Don. Apart from that, however, consumers don't find modern retail banks especially "trustable," he says.

"The ideal customer experience is frictionless," says Don. "There's a lot of research showing that customer satisfaction is not well correlated with customer loyalty. But the research also shows that dissatisfaction correlates highly with disloyalty."

In other words, providing decent customer service is not enough to ensure customer loyalty. But providing bad service almost guarantees customer defections.

Why is this meaningful? Because according to Don, the ideal frictionless interaction includes four attributes:

1. It is reliable.
2. It is relevant to the customer.
3. It is valuable to the customer.
4. It is trustable.

"It doesn't have to be the cheapest on the block, but it must be on a par with its competitive set. It cannot be over-priced relative to the quality of the offering," says Don. "It cannot contain pricing tricks or hidden fees. It has to be simple and straightforward."

From my perspective, the most important takeaway from the interview with Don was the idea of trustability, which he defines as "proactive trustworthiness," meaning that the service provider goes above and beyond what is customarily expected. The example Don uses is Amazon, which alerts customers immediately if they are poised to buy a book that they have already purchased.

"Amazon could easily make more money by selling me another copy of a book that I already own," says Don. "But Amazon understands that my trust and confidence are worth more to them in the long term than the profit they would earn from a single transaction."

It would not have been cheating or even deceptive for Amazon just to send the book. But if your goal is establishing trust, then you must elevate your game to the next level and proactively warn your customers when they are about to make a mistake or do something that's not in their best interests.

"That's what I love about Amazon," says Don. "And the amazing thing is that it's not even a human that's looking out for my interests; it's a computer running a program. I'm in love with a line of code!"

Don's larger point—that banks must resist the urge to profit from the mistakes of their customers—is well taken. It's fair to say that if we want to compete in the era of mobility, we need to upgrade the quality of our customer relationships.

When we asked Don to pick a winner in the looming battle for mobile banking customers, this was his reply: "If I had to place a bet, I would bet on a large, digitally savvy company that does not have the word *bank* in its name today."

Over the Horizon

In many parts of the economy, cash is quickly becoming obsolete. Checks are next on the extinction list. The likely end game is some kind of mobile wallet, but we're not there yet. Prepaid cards represent a logical intermediate step on the path from cash to checking to mobile banking. My guess is that plastic prepaid cards will evolve into mobile prepaid cards much more quickly than anyone expects. Maybe it will happen in five years, maybe in 10 years. But it will be sooner rather than later.

I don't see the problem as plastic cards versus mobile devices. I see an evolution in which a mobile solution gradually becomes as usable and as practical as a plastic card. At that point, a plastic card will feel redundant and people will simply stop carrying them.

Most of us already feel as though we are carrying too many cards, and we feel lost without our mobile phones. I'm betting that mobile transactions will become the norm fairly quickly.

Notes

1. *Sources:* MasterCard, Mercator, SGS Analysis.
2. Don Peppers and Martha Rogers, *Extreme Trust: Honesty as a Competitive Advantage* (New York: Portfolio, 2012).

CHAPTER 7

Risks, Problems, and Headaches

Know What You're Getting Into

At this point, let's hear from Annetta Cortez, an experienced and respected risk management consultant to the financial services industry. From Annetta's perspective, the main risks of mobile banking are similar to the risks associated with Internet banking.

Here is Annetta's quick list of main risks, and it is worth reviewing:

- *Phishing*. This usually involves a fake link or fake request for login information.
- *Identity theft*. Identity theft is usually done on the back of phishing, when other personal information is stolen, rather than simply the direct theft of money.
- *Keylogging*. This is notably done when different systems are used—such as in an Internet café. The computer captures what is being typed. In this context it is not a threat for mobile devices. However, malware may be used that creates a similar threat on the mobile device.
- *Pharming*. This happens when a bank's URL is hijacked and the consumer is redirected to a fake site. Similar issues can happen on mobile devices when fake apps are provided.

- *Malware*. Mentioned earlier, this is a more general term for the kind of programs that can create security problems. Mostly this is spyware and, in the case of mobile banking, SMS Trojans. Any of the previously listed issues can be delivered via malware.
- *Malicious applications*. These are generally the mechanisms by which the malware is delivered. They include fake apps that carry malware with them or that use other mechanisms to scam the user.
- *Privacy violations*. Privacy violations relative to application collection and distribution of data can be due to malware or due to applications taking a more expansive view of data privacy. A more common issue with mobile devices is that users are often carrying them across borders and so run a risk of violating different laws in different countries. Many countries now have laws restricting the porting of consumer information outside of the country.
- *Loss or theft*. Because these are personal devices, mobile devices tend to have more information stored on them—so they tend to have more credit card and password information stored within. They are also lost more readily. So it is important for consumers to manage this information more carefully and for banks and other vendors (such as wireless carriers) to provide rapid shutdown services. Many more inexperienced vendors will not have developed the processes and skill sets to support this.
- *Wireless carrier infrastructure vulnerabilities*. Security weaknesses in this chain can put the customer's data at risk. Although quite possible and reasonably natural for governments to tap information in this way, it is less common as a threat to mobile banking.
- *Payments infrastructure/ecosystem vulnerabilities*. Point-of-sale (POS) threats emerge where there are potential weaknesses in the system. This is particularly important regarding

the more futuristic uses of mobile banking and banking applications to reach the underbanked. MasterCard and PayPal, as well as another venture between Visa and Fundamo, are developing instant secure payment applications that have similarities to debit cards. Some companies are looking at chip- and PIN-related technologies with capabilities resident within the phone. Right now, those projects are more in the planning stages, but that is where the more interesting changes in the industry are likely to emerge.

- *SMS vulnerabilities.* Redirection, hijacking, and spoofing are usually related to malware attacks.
- *Hardware and operating system vulnerabilities.* There is some concern regarding the reliability of devices, wireless connections, and so on, and the issues that can arise because of these. In my view, although the problems may be more frequent than in a standard computer scenario, they are similar enough. But here again, those who have experience with Internet banking or related services will have a leg up on those who do not have this experience.
- *Complex supply chain and new entrants into the mobile ecosystem.* As discussed, this is primarily related to the payment system issues. New entrants are likely to come along via phone companies, telecoms, or other types of relationships.
- *Lack of maturity of antifraud tools and controls.* Related to the issues at the top of the list, there is a view that because of the mobile nature and speed of transaction, coupled with wireless issues, there needs to be further development of tools and controls in this area.

"A lot depends on which side you're on—in other words, whether you are a provider or a consumer," says Annetta. "If you are a consumer, the biggest risk is losing your device or having it stolen. It's far easier to lose or misplace a mobile phone than it is to lose or misplace a laptop or a PC."

Since consumers typically want to reduce the number of steps required to log into an account through a mobile app, they are less likely to implement multiple layers of security. Fewer layers of security can make it easier for a thief to gain access to someone's account information.

"That's probably the single biggest risk for the consumer—simply losing the device and having someone hack into your accounts," says Annetta. "If you've configured your device to require the minimum security and it is lost or stolen, then you are in trouble."

From the provider's side, it's also an issue, because consumers naturally expect their providers to offer some kind of security to minimize the inherent risks. That ups the ante for providers.

"If you're offering mobile banking services, then you have to figure out how to handle those sorts of situations where customers lose their devices," says Annetta. "There are a number of security solutions out there, such as key fobs,[1] but they're not widely utilized by consumers. If you're offering mobile banking in a mass market scenario, you have to consider the trade-offs between convenience and security. Some consumers might not think that key fobs are particularly convenient. But if you're a bank, you're probably thinking that greater convenience can translate into greater risk."

In the short term, added security means less convenience. That's a fact that marketers will simply have to accept. However, vendors of security solutions will see the emergence of mobile banking as a business opportunity, and will compete to provide the most effective and most convenient solutions to the market.

"We're seeing a lot of forays into new and improved technologies for increasing the security of mobile devices," says Annetta. "Some of the companies that pioneered security for Internet banking are seeing similar opportunities for mobile banking. We're also seeing new vendors break into this space, and hopefully there will be a lively competition to see who comes up with the next great security solution for mobile banking."

Although device security is a significant issue, the overarching risk for banks is the potential loss of customers and market share as nonbank entities enter the mobile banking market.

"Loss of market share is a fundamentally strategic risk," says Annetta. "Technology companies will develop solutions for managing device risks. But the real risks are far deeper. As mobile banking gains acceptance, it threatens the whole idea of having branch networks. Banks have already adapted their branch operations to keep up with changing consumer habits, but the rise of mobile banking will force them to evolve even faster. Banks will have to accept the fact that a lot of people are never going to walk into a branch."

I think the question raised by Annetta boils down to whether banks are willing to make the investments necessary for serving customers who never visit their branches.

And if banks are not willing to make those investments, will they lose their customers to nonbank players—such as telecoms and retailers—who are ready to pony up big bucks to create new markets for themselves?

"When you have telecoms, device makers, and retailers thinking about penetrating the consumer banking market, traditional banks have to view that as strategic risk," says Annetta.

That said, consumer banking as we know it is not likely to disappear overnight. "I don't see banks losing their core lending business," says Annetta. She does not envision nonbank entities usurping traditional banks as providers of car loans and mortgages. Mobile banking might be able to handle some kinds of small-scale loans, but making larger loans will still require the infrastructure of a traditional bank, she says.

"For amounts that you would put on a credit card, I can see mobile-only companies making those kinds of loans. For anything larger, I think you're going to need a real bank," says Annetta.

From her perspective as a risk management expert, Annetta sees mobile banking as a place for small-scale, relatively simple consumer transactions. "Remember, the minute you get into anything requiring a deposit, you're talking about having a banking license. And when you have a banking license, your life gets much more difficult," she says.

As technology evolves and markets become more millennial-centric, all of those assumptions are likely to change. For the time being and immediate future, however, Annetta sees a series of gradual shifts rather than seismic changes.

"Here's my informal and unofficial advice for anyone trying to enter the mobile banking arena: Number 1, you're not likely to succeed in mobile banking unless you already have a strong Internet banking presence. I don't think it would be a good idea to leap into mobile banking if you haven't already perfected your ability to offer Internet banking. Number 2, you must be prepared to address consumer security issues. If you don't have a security solution in place, you will face huge risks, both financial and reputational. Number 3, you must understand the competitive field and know who the players are. If you're a bank, you might consider partnering with a telecom, or if you're a telecom, you might consider partnering with a bank."

Don't Restrict Finance to the Desktop

Kurt Schneiber is a former Citibank colleague, and a great all-around guy. He served recently as CEO and acting chairman at Syncada, a global financial supply chain network processing an average of $20 billion in payments per year. Kurt was recruited as CEO to orchestrate the build-out and global scaling of the early-stage joint venture into a sustainable international financial services business with the underlying complexity of supply chain finance, and as acting chair of the board of directors to ensure alignment of joint venture partners on key strategic issues. He also served on the board as compensation committee chair and finance committee chair. Kurt is someone who really knows his way around the finance industry, and I am delighted to include his insights in the book.

I asked Kurt to chat with me about the risks and rewards of mobile banking. Here are some of his responses.

"Bankers will need to be more responsive and become better listeners in order to provide the needed services in a competitively friendly fashion to consumers of all stripes," says Kurt. "Switching costs for those who buy banking services are extremely low, and competitive options are presented consistently, making the option to switch simple. In addition, clearinghouse web applications allow consumers to shop for banking services just like they shop for airline fares, hotel rooms, or credit cards. If banks are not at the right place at the right time and with competitive and compelling services through the right medium, then they will find their business eroding."

I also asked Kurt how he sees mobile technology changing the payments and credit industries. His reply is instructive and useful:

"Access to choice and the option to shift will continue to increase. Those providing banking and credit services will of necessity be shut out of the consumer's choices if they do not present themselves where and when the consumer of these services wants to make decisions," says Kurt.

Well, there you have it. Bankers and providers of financial services need to be where their customers are. If their customers are working from their desktops or laptops, that's fine. But as more customers migrate to their business activities to their mobile devices, you'd better be ready. Many of today's customers will use whichever device is at hand, and my guess is they don't really care if it's a PC or a mobile tablet. For most people, a screen is a screen, whether it's on their laptop or their smartphone. This is even true as you move deeper into the business. "Those who manage the financial supply chain and the associated physical supply chain expect to be able to respond to opportunities quickly. Restricting transactional capabilities to the desktop—when a desk may not even exist for some key managers—will force consumers of these services and capabilities to go elsewhere. Visibility to the flow of funds at all times by the right people, in supply chain and treasury, will be a standard requirement. Interoperability will also be key," says Kurt.

Those are important messages that we should all consider and absorb. When you're running a bank, you have "customers" all around you, and at every level of the organization. The people working for you behind the scenes probably feel the same way about their mobile devices as the consumers you see at your branches. Everyone is thinking the same thought: *Why can't I just do this on my phone?*

Forty Years in the Desert?

Steve Smith is an experienced bank card executive with international experience. Steve works with leading card issuers worldwide, developing and implementing solutions in a variety of areas, including credit and debit card business strategy, co-branding, product development, customer and financial management, customer service, and sales training.

Steve cautions against developing or emerging economies jumping right into the most mature card market initiatives (such as cobranding and mobile payments) before their management skills, infrastructure, and regulatory frameworks have had the opportunity to develop—and before their customers gain a mature understanding of how and when to use a card.

He offers the U.S. credit card industry as an example of a relatively mature industry in which the major players have lived through a continuing series of ups and downs spanning the decades since cards were introduced. "With the benefit of experience, U.S. issuers have developed perspective (i.e., don't panic!) and risk management tools (e.g., models and monitoring routines) to minimize losses and maximize recovery."

Steve compares established card issuers to Moses, who trekked through the desert for 40 years before arriving at the Promised Land. "An old generation died and a new one was born during those 40 years," says Steve. "I'm concerned that some of the emerging markets are trying to skip from today to tomorrow without going through that generational change first."

He also expresses concern that some banks might be moving too quickly into newer technologies such as mobile because they want to appear cool to their younger customers. That's a mistake, says Steve. "Don't pretend to be cool if you aren't. Don't do things that are inconsistent with your brand or your image."

There aren't many examples of traditional banks that have moved successfully into mobile banking, he notes. Partnering with companies that already have mobile expertise is one way for establishing banks to move smoothly into the mobile space. But it's not clear which companies make the best natural partners.

"If you partner with a telecom company, then it's another hand in the pot. The telecom will need a share of the profit," says Steve. "But no bank really wants to give up what is an increasingly thin profit to begin with. The banks are reluctant to enter partnerships without clearly understanding the value added. And I don't think there's a consensus among banks on the value added by partnerships in that area."

Partnering with companies such as MasterCard and Visa, however, might seem less risky to banks, since they already perceive MasterCard and Visa more as natural partners than as competitors, Steve explains.

"The banks might be skeptical of partnerships with Master-Card and Visa, but they will be more open to listening to them than to the telecoms," says Steve. "But it's hard to tell who the best partners will be, because that would require the ability to see into the future. The tech industry has demonstrated that things can change very quickly. Banks, on the other hand, are accustomed to moving more slowly. People are afraid that Google or Apple will disrupt everything tomorrow. There's no certainty about what will happen, which explains why many banks seem like deer caught in headlights. They're waiting to see what happens."

To a certain extent, Steve believes that the fuss over mobile banking and mobile payments is much ado about nothing. "I'm somewhat nonplussed by the whole thing," he says. "Credit cards *are* mobile payments. I don't think that consumers are half as interested in all of this as the media is. To them, it's mostly invisible."

From Steve's perspective, the most interesting aspect of the developing mobile economy—and perhaps also the riskiest—is that mobile payments will make credit cards truly invisible. "Your credit card is already invisible to you when you're buying some-thing on Amazon or when you reload your Starbucks card. How will that invisibility change everyone's thinking? How will it affect acquisition, retention, and attrition? That's the question nobody seems to be asking. To me, that is the most interesting part."

Mobile Apps Are Not Manufactured

Greg Fell is the former CIO of Terex, a Fortune 500 maker of heavy equipment. Since 2013, he has served as chief strategy officer of Crisply, a big data start-up that tracks billable hours. He began his IT career at Ford Motor Company, and has a wealth of experience managing complex software development projects. Greg is also the author of *Decoding the IT Value Problem*,[2] an excellent book that looks beneath the layers of hype that often make it difficult for top executives to make good decisions about technology investments.

A useful chunk of advice from Greg's book that I took to heart is his admonition not to think of software development—including mobile app development—as a form of manufacturing.

"There is an unfortunate tendency . . . to perceive software development as a manufacturing process," writes Greg. "The perception that software development (SWD) operates by the same principles as manufacturing processes leads to mistaken assumptions, false beliefs, and disappointing outcomes. To be blunt, SWD is not a manufacturing process."

Greg notes correctly that software development "is an engineering and innovation process. It is invention at its very core. By definition, anything that has to be developed doesn't exist. Things that don't exist are far less predictable than things that just need to be assembled. That's an extremely important concept that is often lost."

While small-scale projects "that replicate commonly understood processes are easy to manage because most of the work involves re-using existing code," most software development projects do not fall into that category, according to Greg.

"Most . . . projects require iterative steps of invention and testing. Testing is time consuming, but it is my belief that most failures of technology can be traced back to inadequate testing. In my experience, most problems can be caught and fixed with proper testing," writes Greg.

Here is the heart of Greg's concern: "When time is short, testing phases are often skipped or shortened. People cross their fingers and hope for the best. That is not a good strategy."

As Greg rightly observes, "Good programming teams measure and monitor their work to understand where they are on the development cycle. They don't test too much, and they don't test too little. They find the right balance."

Greg cautions his readers to remember that software errors are like typing errors, and that even the best typists occasionally hit the wrong key. "The simple truth is that the more you type, the more mistakes you will make. The same holds true for software code," writes Greg. "The longer the program, the more errors it will contain. That is why you need to test software before it goes into production."

Greg makes a strong and eloquent case for testing your apps thoroughly before launching. That said, at some point you just have to launch the service. If you've done your testing beforehand, the chances are good that you'll be able to fix any glitches or problems that arise without jeopardizing the success of your project.

Think Globally, Act Locally

My friend Harvey Koeppel was CIO of Citibank's Global Consumer Group during a period of rapid expansion into growth markets in Asia. As a key player and senior executive at Citibank, he was often at the center of the storm, and he has a truly unique perspective on the risks and rewards of opening new markets.

Harvey was a leader in Citibank's 2005 effort to create a mobile banking system in India, so he has plenty of on-the-ground experience to draw upon. I caught up with Harvey recently in New York City, and asked him to share some of what he learned from his experiences at Citibank.

"If you are a U.S.-based bank looking to create a larger global footprint and expand your business in other countries, particularly in global growth markets, first and foremost you need to make sure that you understand the local banking culture, the local customs, the regulatory environment, and the competition," says Harvey.

Understanding the differences and similarities between U.S. and foreign markets is absolutely essential for success, he says. For example, Citibank quickly discovered that speaking face-to-face with a loan officer was an uncomfortable experience for many Japanese consumers, which made it difficult for the bank to expand its consumer lending business in Japan.

"We came up with a very interesting idea, which was a kiosk that enabled customers to enter information, scan documents, and complete their loan application without having to sit across a desk from a loan officer," says Harvey. "The kiosks were like ATMs, and consumers were comfortable using them. In this instance, depersonalizing the process proved helpful. We called the kiosks ALM, short for automated lending machines, and they were quite successful."

Harvey's story illustrates the value of understanding the difference between markets and of tailoring product offerings and services to accommodate local preferences.

For example, the ability to exchange foreign currencies freely and easily is considered incredibly important in many emerging markets and developing economies. "So if you were a U.S. bank doing business in Asia or Africa, you would need to offer currency exchange services to your local customers," he says. "In many countries around the world, currency exchange isn't something unusual or exotic—it's a regular part of doing business."

Whenever possible, mobile banking initiatives will have to play by local rules and provide services that local markets expect and demand. "To that end, it makes sense to partner with local firms. You will need to work with people who really know the local culture, local habits, and local laws," says Harvey. "Knowing what time most people arrive for work, when they take their siestas, and when they go home at the end of their workday can make the difference between success and failure."

If you are a large bank entering a new market, you are likely to face competition from established local firms. "More than likely, you will be viewed with a degree of skepticism and in some cases, with outright contempt. That's why you need to understand the local culture and try your best to fit in smoothly. At a minimum, you'll have language issues to overcome, which is another reason to partner with local firms," he says.

Harvey raised another area of concern, which is data storage. "Many countries have stringent laws about where the data can be kept and maintained. Often there are prohibitions against personal and financial data leaving the country. Switzerland would be an obvious case. Germany also has strict laws regarding data storage and transfer," says Harvey. "The point is that different countries have different laws, and if you're designing a mobile banking system, you want to make sure that it can operate legally in all the countries where you plan to offer it."

I asked Harvey to envision a scenario in which he was asked to build a mobile banking system from the ground up. Here is his response: "I would partner with a telecom in the country where I was going to operate the system. I would find the largest and least expensive mobile provider and create a partnership. Mobile banking depends on mobile connectivity. That's why I would partner with a telecom."

The Role of the CIO in Mobile Banking

Harvey also told me that he learned some important lessons about the critical role of the CIO in technology-enabled business initiatives. "As the CIO, you have to understand how the business works. You need to be responsive to the business when it asks for a particular kind of technology, but you also need to be aware of newer and alternative technologies that people aren't necessarily talking about," says Harvey.

"Good CIOs use those newer technologies to drive business value and to create new products with sustainable revenue streams," says Harvey. "When you're the CIO, you're right at the intersection of business and technology. Your job is finding and applying the right technology that will enable the business to achieve its goals."

It seems logical to assume that CIOs will have to become more adept at managing the people, processes, and technologies associated with mobile business. They will also need to hire top talent with expertise in the various facets of mobile technology, from infrastructure architecture to application development.

Big box retailers aren't waiting for banks to lead the way. "Some of the larger retails let you sign up for a program where they'll send a discount coupon to your mobile device when you're within a quarter-mile of a store. The enabling technology is called 'geo-fencing,' and it basically tells them when a customer is nearby. That whole idea of knowing where the customer is and marketing directly to the customer when he or she is near the store is revolutionizing consumer businesses," says Harvey.

Will banks join the revolution, or will they wait for a perfect moment that might never arrive? Harvey is optimistic, but he also has his doubts. "Banks have historically been slow to adopt new technologies. Bankers tend to be risk averse, which goes with the territory. When you throw a global financial crisis on top of their inherent distaste for risk, it can be difficult to get technology projects going," he says.

"But as the general economy continues growing, my guess is that some banks will become more willing to try new things and invest more money in newer technologies," says Harvey. "My hunch is that mobile banking isn't a fad and that sooner or later, all banks will embrace it."

I certainly admire Harvey's candor. His insight has the ring of truth, and it will be interesting to see which banks jump into the swimming pool and which stay in their lounge chairs until the last possible moment.

Notes

1. According to Webopedia, a key fob is "a small security hardware device with built-in authentication used to control and secure access to network services and data. The key fob displays a randomly generated access code, which changes periodically, usually every 30 to 60 seconds. A user first authenticates [one-self] on the key fob with a personal identification number (PIN), followed by the current code displayed on the device."
2. Gregory J. Fell, *Decoding the IT Value Problem: An Executive Guide for Achieving Optimal ROI on Critical IT Investments* (Hoboken, NJ: John Wiley & Sons, 2013).

CHAPTER 8

Mobile Everything

The Doctor Will See You Now . . .

As the old saying goes, "What good is money without health?" Surely it will be wonderful to perform a wide range of financial transactions on our mobile devices, but what difference will it make if we aren't healthy enough to enjoy the benefits and conveniences afforded by our cool new technologies?

That's why the promise of mobile health care is so alluring. It offers the vision of achieving wellness and health without spending lots of time in the doctor's office, waiting to be examined. Imagine a world in which not only your mobile phone, but also your wristwatch, your clothing, your contact lenses, and even your toothbrush continuously help you monitor your health and collect critical data about your medical conditions.

In a truly connected mobile economy, doctors' offices would become as obsolete as bank branches. The need for them would simply cease to exist because all the information your doctor would need to know about you and your condition in order to make the right diagnosis, recommend treatment, and prescribe the proper medication or therapy would be available through a mobile telecommunications network.

"Until the widespread adoption of mobile technology, we had to be physically present in front of a PC or laptop to access relevant information. At worst, we had to wait to get home to access the Internet via the PC, and at best, we had to lug around a laptop. Now, the mobile phone serves as the interface, so we can have access to information anytime, anywhere, via a lightweight device, which we all carry anyway. So we can access health information and resources freely," says Narayanan Ram, CEO of PurpleTeal, a U.S.-based health messaging services provider.

From Narayanan's point of view, the most exciting aspect of mobile health care is education. "By making people more aware of their health risks, we can prompt them to take preventive action," he says. "And we can help people do a better job of managing their conditions and avoiding complications."

Mobile health care delivery would be incalculably valuable in emerging and developing parts of the world where travel is difficult and doctors are scarce. Imagine the number of lives that could be saved if people didn't have to cross rivers, climb mountains, or travel for days every time they needed help from a health care professional.

The idea that doctors will examine, diagnose, prescribe, and follow up with patients via mobile devices is not a wild-eyed fantasy. It's an entirely reasonable vision that will be achieved in stages. A fully functional and totally integrated mobile health care experience won't happen tomorrow, but it will happen over the next decade. When it arrives in full bloom, mobile health care will have an enormous impact on all of us.

Before moving on, let's spend a moment discussing the semantics of the term *mobile health care*. From my perspective, mobile health care is to health care what mobile banking is to banking—it's a technology that allows consumers to access health care services from digital devices (e.g., PCs, tablets, smartphones, etc.) without having to visit a health care provider.

Matthew Holt, a widely quoted health care technology guru, bristles when he hears the term *mobile health care*, because it suggests a system dominated by cell phones. As Matt rightly points out, mobile health care is more likely to be a system of systems, a platform supporting multiple technologies, networks, and interfaces. In other words, in the mobile health care universe, BYOD (bring your own device) will be the norm. Matt refers to the emerging health care platform as the "health interface layer." I like that name, and I hope it sticks.

What's the Business Model?

Let's look at some of the challenges and opportunities as they exist today. First of all, there are likely to be several classes or types of mobile health care apps: one kind for patients, another kind for clinicians, and probably a third kind for researchers collecting data. Each class or type of mobile app will likely have its own unique set of qualities and attributes.

On September 25, 2103, the U.S. Department of Health and Human Services, the Food and Drug Administration (FDA), the Center for Devices and Radiological Health, and the Center for Biologics Evaluation and Research issued a comprehensive list of nonbinding recommendations for mobile medical applications.[1] The 43-page document offers guidance for industry and FDA staff, and it strongly suggests that the government will not sit idly by as mobile health care devices are developed and marketed.

In the absence of a government-led project to create a viable ecosystem of mobile health care apps, it's fair to assume that the vast majority of mobile health care apps will be developed by the market, which means that the people or corporations who invest in the development of those apps will expect them to earn a profit at some point.

So perhaps the first logical question to ask is: "What does the business model for a mobile health care app look like?" The answer will undoubtedly depend on whether the app is intended for use by clinicians, patients, researchers, or other types of users.

Aligning Technology with Plan Incentives

Since most health care costs are paid for by insurers and indirectly by employers, it seems fair to say that the health care insurance industry and major employer groups will play a significant role in determining the success or failure of many mobile health care apps.

"The key is aligning technology adoption with plan incentives," says Stan Nowak, CEO and cofounder of Silverlink, a leader in driving consumer health engagement. Stan, who has an undergraduate degree from Harvard College and an MBA from Harvard Business School, says mobile health care entrepreneurs can learn valuable lessons from existing corporate health care management programs designed to help employees quit smoking, lose weight, manage chronic illness, and become more physically fit.

"Innovation in this category tends to come from self-insured employers, because they have a long-term interest in their employees, and the economics of health insurance haven't traditionally supported significant incentives. Further, the incentive structures that work best tend to be embedded in the plan design, rather than discrete incentive events," according to Stan.

"It's fairly obvious that if you're delivering a plan design, including meaningful incentives to maintain a healthy weight, for example, you need education, trackable measures, and a way to engage employees and nudge behavior," says Stan. "All of this is clearly an opportunity for mobile health."

In a sense, we are moving as a culture toward a sort of self-service health care model in which consumers are generally expected to assume more responsibility for monitoring and managing their own health. The general trend toward self-service certainly works in favor of the mobile health care vision described at the beginning of this chapter.

Preventive health and wellness strategies pose intrinsic business challenges because they almost always *save* rather than *generate* money. Let's be perfectly honest: Most business models are built around the idea of *making* money, not saving it. So there's an inherent problem with the whole idea of wellness, at least from the perspective of pure profit motive. How do you make money from keeping people healthy?

If there's anyone on the planet who can offer a reasonable answer to that question, it's Steve Blank. A retired eight-time serial entrepreneur-turned-educator and author, Steve has changed how start-ups are built and how entrepreneurship is taught around the globe. Steve is the author of the best-selling *The Startup Owner's Manual*, and his earlier seminal work, *The Four Steps to the Epiphany*, is credited with launching the lean start-up movement. His May 2013 *Harvard Business Review* article on lean start-ups defined the movement.

Mike Barlow, who served as editorial director and producer of this book project, spoke with him recently, and here are key excerpts of Steve's insight into the digital health movement:

> *Mobile technology puts information at the fingertips of doctors. It's a key enabler in "personalized" or "precision" medicine that allows the integration of not only a particular patient's medical records from electronic medical records, but also the integration of that patient's records with the sum of all external knowledge about a disease or finding.*
>
> *A clinician looking at a patient can now compare that patient with thousands, or tens of thousands, or millions of other patients, and have the sum of all the diagnoses and treatment options right at his or her fingertips.*

119

For consumers, mobile will let you look up your own symptoms, check your own blood pressure, send data to your glucose meter, et cetera.

The problem is that naive digital health start-ups don't understand that once you start doing diagnoses or offering advice, you run head-on into some very, very strict regulations in the United States. The FDA just issued guidance on mobile medical devices . . . the good news is that in the long run, consumers will be better off with the FDA involved. In the short term, however, it will be a real food fight.

Digital health start-ups are started either by health care entrepreneurs or by technology entrepreneurs. It's like two mints in one. You're either coming from the health care side or you're coming from the technology side.

The health care entrepreneurs think that if they build something, it will sell itself; that if doctors recommend something, patients will use it; and that if a clinical trial proves something is effective, it will automatically become a successful product in the market.

Technology entrepreneurs think that insurance companies will pay for products because patients want them, or that the patients will pay the costs themselves. They also think that all they need to do is plug into the hospitals' electronic medical records.

As it turns out, both the health care entrepreneurs and the technology entrepreneurs are mistaken.

Start-ups fail in this digital health area for three main reasons: One, they have a poor understanding of the customer. Two, it costs them more to acquire customers than those customers are worth in terms of lifetime value, and they have limited access to high-quality distribution channels. Three, they have flawed revenue strategies, which is a fancy way of saying they didn't quite figure out how to make money.

120

It turns out that digital health is not just the intersection of health care and technology—it's creating a unique domain.

I love this idea of a "unique domain" because it seems to strike at the heart of the problem. Digital or mobile health care poses challenges that are very different from the challenges posed separately by health care and information technology.

Steve suggests looking at the emerging digital health care space as a Venn diagram with two overlapping circles, one representing health care and the other representing information technology. The overlap, or the intersection, is the unique domain of digital health care.

In the health care circle, you have topics like customer segments, coverage, reimbursement, providers, clinical trial design, and quality outcomes. In the IT circle, you have topics like commerce, economics, revenue strategies, consumer apps, user interface designs, and mobile metrics.

But what's unique in the intersection between the two circles are customer value propositions, analytics, retention tools, distribution channels, data partners, patient social networks, and regulations. The digital health space is creating a whole new set of unique activities that you have to figure out.

Steve recommends that entrepreneurs in the emerging digital health care space avoid repeating mistakes made by entrepreneurs in the clean technology or clean tech space, in which billions of dollars were essentially wasted.

There is no such thing as clean tech. You could be doing semiconductor solar cells, wastewater treatment, or batteries. You could be doing solar panel installations. Those are all very different business models with different customers and different channels. If you didn't understand those subtleties, you went out of business.

Steve seems generally optimistic about the future of digital health care, but he's far too experienced to gloss over the complexity of challenges and the importance of getting the business models right.

If you are considering launching a business in the digital health care space, I urge you to read Steve's excellent post, "Reinventing Life Science Startups—Medical Devices and Digital Health."[2] I also recommend reading his "Lessons Learned in Digital Health."[3] You can find them, along with many other excellent articles and resources, on his blog. Just point your browser to http://steveblank.com and you can access Steve's incredibly useful insights directly.

Evolving Interfaces

Jonathan Teich, MD, PhD, is chief medical informatics officer at Elsevier, and a physician at Brigham and Women's Hospital in Boston, Massachusetts. His areas of expertise include health information infrastructure, e-prescribing, and clinical decision support systems. His primary focus lies in the design of innovative information systems to directly improve clinical care, prevent adverse events, and streamline clinical work flow to address the most critical needs of the health care community.

He sees a system of mobile medical devices emerging "organically" over time. We spoke with him recently, and here are edited excerpts from our conversation:

I think that the interfaces tend to still be evolving. If you look at popular applications from five years ago compared to today, they have changed—just like design has changed and fonts on signs have changed, and so on. I think that's still evolving. We have the general expectations, but things continue to be added in. We're seeing a little bit more voice input. We're seeing a little bit more graphical tools. I don't know that the user level is ready to be standardized. I think that's something that evolves as design and freshness take over.

The question really is whether we will see standards for these applications to exchange data with each other. Will it be possible for a bunch of different health care applications to interconnect so that a diet application can connect to a food shopping application, which can connect to a banking application? What can we do to make these things talk to each other? Will there be safe/secure ways for my electronic health record in a hospital to convey certain pieces of information to me on my device?

I think that's where the standardization will be very much welcomed: at the infrastructure level and the interface level from one app to another. We'd love to see a world where there are a lot of these things and we can interconnect them like LEGO pieces, appropriately and correctly, to make a much better application than you began with.

We asked Dr. Teich to describe an idealized scenario in which he could use the various components of a mobile health care delivery system in real life. His reply was illuminating, and hopeful:

As a professional, I look forward to a time not very far away, when I'm doing an exam or a procedure as a physician and where I realize that I need to know something, that I can ask the mobile device a question and have the question answered in just the way that I need, and that the device can even guide me to a particular electronic helper or assistant that I need to help me.

It may even get to the point where the device knows a little bit about what I'm doing because it's tracking my movements or sensing something in the room. Sooner or later we'll get to the tricorder,[4] but I think that's still a little way off.

A Practical Framework for Patient Self-Management

We had a wonderful conversation recently with Dr. Neal Kaufman, the cofounder and chief medical officer of DPS Health, a pioneer in the application of online and mobile technology to help patients cope with the effects of chronic health problems such as obesity, diabetes, and heart disease. Specifically, DPS Health provides technology solutions that address the increasing costs associated with unhealthy patient behaviors.

From Dr. Kaufman's perspective, there are four key approaches for improving the health of patients:

1. Personal health care services (e.g., seeing your doctor)
2. Public health initiatives and laws (antismoking regulations, taxes on liquor and on cigarettes)
3. Population health (analyzing risk factors and outcomes among large groups of patients and providing targeted intervention to those who need it)
4. Direct-to-consumer products and services that enable patients to assume a larger role in managing their health

Although information technology is essential to each of those four approaches, it is an absolutely critical piece of any plan or program that aims to promote and encourage patient self-management. This is a point that seems obvious, but is often overlooked. In other words, you need modern information technology to make self-management a viable option for patients.

"I am convinced that that is the transition period that will lead to major transformations of health care delivery," says Dr. Kaufman.

He writes convincingly about the ways in which technology helps patients assume more active roles in managing their health. Here is an excerpt from one his recent articles that I found particularly insightful:

You may already be familiar with the buzzwords "patient self-management." In layman's terms, it means you have the opportunity to take an active role—in tandem with your healthcare provider—in the treatment of your disease. Today, patient self-management enabled by information technology (websites, email, text messaging, smart phone apps, videos, and more) is becoming an important factor in the way clinicians deliver healthcare and lifestyle support.

Your physician can now provide you with technology-driven education and support programs that are directly linked to a clinician, diabetes educator, or dietician to help you better manage your diabetes and support your need to change unhealthy behaviors for the long-term. These innovative, clinician-linked programs are a coordinated approach to promoting healthy lifestyle that will likely be reimbursed with the new healthcare reform legislation that has recently been approved in the U.S.

The best technology-driven patient self-management programs are rich in relevant content, provide engaging interactive elements, and offer a tailored, personalized learning experience. They contain self-assessment and goal-setting tools, and ways for you to monitor your performance as well as changes in your biologic measurements such as weight, blood pressure, and blood sugar. They also allow you to easily access your information, input your data, and receive support in real-time.

With technology-based learning programs, you can gain knowledge, obtain support, and track your behaviors 24/7. Additionally, a nurse or diabetes educator can serve as a "virtual coach," supporting you in the process and helping you sustain new healthy behaviors.

Of course, technology-enabled behavior change is a complex undertaking. To be successful, technology-based programs must be based on evidence, proven by research, and solidly grounded in behavior change theory and clinical expertise.

The technology doesn't have to be super-sexy or even cutting-edge. In many situations, ordinary text messaging will do fine. Here's more from Dr. Kaufman:

[T]here are a growing number of text messaging–based programs that allow you to receive condition-specific questions, messages, and prompts texted to your phone—and help you communicate via text with peers who have similar health concerns and lifestyle goals. One example, "Diabetes Buddies," developed by DPS Health and being researched in South Africa by UCLA, offers peer-to-peer support through text messaging.

The use of information technology to support patient self-management is becoming an integral part of delivering healthcare and lifestyle support. Today, clinicians can use information technology approaches, coupled with traditional treatment, to support large numbers of patients with diabetes in an economical and practical manner.

Dr. Kaufman also writes about the ways in which online and mobile channels have "created a new role for diabetes educators," enabling them to serve "as a virtual coach efficiently providing individualized, online guidance and support based on readily available analyses of each patient's characteristics and performance. In addition, co-coaches can monitor virtual support groups where patients interact with others online via monitored chat rooms and blogs."[5]

Additionally, he writes, "By incorporating web-based patient self-management and support into traditional treatment approaches, one educator can effectively support many patients—one patient at a time." That is an absolutely critical takeaway: the idea that with modern information technology, we can leverage our vast stores of knowledge to help individual patients!

Here's an excerpt from a recent article Dr. Kaufman wrote for *AADE in Practice*, a publication of the American Association of Diabetes Educators:

For example, to serve large numbers of overweight and sedentary patients, researchers from the University of Pittsburgh worked with DPS Health to transform the landmark Diabetes Prevention Program (DPP) into an online intervention called Virtual Lifestyle Management (VLM). The DPP is a weight management approach developed by the University of Pittsburgh under a federal research grant from the National Institutes of Health. It proved that overweight and sedentary adults could be counseled to eat better, be more active, and lose weight. To create the VLM service, the University, along with DPS Health, used the principles of the DPP to develop a yearlong, engaging, web-based learning, motivating, educating, goal setting, and tracking intervention. Through VLM, patients with or at risk for type 2 diabetes improve their physical activity and nutrition habits and sustain these new behaviors. VLM increases educator efficiency by automating patient learning, planning, self-monitoring, and encouragement, and helps the educator efficiently provide patient support through limited personalized electronic coaching.

127

I'm impressed by Dr. Kaufman's real-world experience and clear-eyed responses. He also raises another important point that I want to share with you. For many "m-health" businesses, the dominant approach is "identifying individuals who are already in pretty good health or at fairly low risk, and helping them exercise more efficiently or run a faster 10K race," notes Dr. Kaufman. "That's fine, but it's not going to improve long-term health outcomes or bend the cost curve of health care."

That is a really great observation, and I'm glad that Dr. Kaufman brought it into the conversation. If you're already healthy, mobile health care can help you become healthier, at least in theory. If you are sick, or if you are managing a chronic condition, mobile health care can potentially mean a lot more. For people with genuine health risks, mobile health care can make a huge difference in the quality of life. If applied broadly across the population, mobile health care has the potential to reduce overall health care costs by billions of dollars, and save or extend millions of lives.

From my perspective, the fundamental benefits of mobile health care would apply in both the developed and the emerging parts of the world. To me, that is a genuinely exciting possibility.

Improving Health Care, One Atom at a Time

Mobile technology will also play in exciting role in the diagnosis and treatment of serious disease using nanotechnology. In the not-too-distant future, we will use our mobile devices to spot tumors and track their growth. We will also use our mobile devices to monitor the progress of the therapies administered by our doctors to cure our illnesses.

I predict that mobile technology will serve as a great equalizer that allows health care services to be delivered more readily and more efficiently, particularly in the developing world. From a health care perspective, mobile will help us bridge the gap between the haves and the have-nots. For example, in India, 90 percent of the neurosurgeons live in cities, while 90 percent of the people live in rural areas. Mobile health care can bring the expertise of specialists and other health care providers to people living in the most remote areas—without making them travel to a city for treatment.

I spoke recently with my friend Ramesh Bhargava, the CEO of Nanocrystals Technology (NCT). According to *Bloomberg Businessweek*, NCT develops and produces nanomaterials based on quantum confined atoms (QCAs). The company's QCA-based technology demonstrates how a single atom, when incorporated in a nanosize-material, results in unique magnetic nanophosphors (MNPs). The applications of MNPs include improved, flat-slim displays, efficient LEDs, and other lighting-devices, magneto-optical memories, contrast agent for MRI, targeted drug-delivery, bio-markers, and more.

Basically, Ramesh and his team at NCT are using nanotech-nology to help us live longer, healthier, and more productive lives. I asked Ramesh a series of questions for this book. Here are the questions and his replies, lightly edited:

1. What Is Nanotechnology?

Nanotechnology enables us to overcome certain "application barriers" that prevent us from developing efficient and novel products. Overcoming the barriers creates a large range of advantages for nanoparticles of certain size, ranging from 10 nm to 60 nm. For example, today's semiconductor industry is using 30 nm size active transistors but simply refer it as submicron technology. The reason being that they do not generate any new properties, except that the number of transistors per area increases as the chip size is decreased, leading to higher speed and density. In true nanotechnology, we not only change the density or communication speed with nano-size but create novel properties that are critically dependent on decreasing size and needs quantum mechanics to explain the resultant properties. For example, we have created weak ferromagnetic material from nonferrous material by introducing a single foreign atom in 5-50 nm size nanoparticles.

2. How will nanotechnology change the future of medicine, health, and wellness?

We are in midst of developing nanoparticles with properties that will help us to diagnose with higher resolution and contrast and enable us to determine precisely the disorder and its location, as well as develop a process that helps to deliver the drug to the target to provide therapeutic advantages. This breakthrough provides something we call theranostics (therapy + diagnostics = theranostics). Our MNPs potentially can yield 20 times better contrast agent in MRI than the currently used contrast agents. This enhanced contrast results in locating ~1mm^3 of cancerous tumor (compared to ~1cm^3 resolution currently possible). For the therapeutic breakthrough, our MNPs when conjugated with drugs, create so-called magnetic drugs. These "magnetic drugs" now can be immobilized at a given target by applying an external magnetic field. This results in simultaneous reduction in toxicity, dosage, and damage to other organs. The theranostics use of nanotechnology is now feasible with the use of our MNPs.

3. How is your company deploying nanotechnology?

NCT has created the first nanomagnet that provides high-resolution, high-contrast diagnostic MRI and also enables to deliver the drug-coated MNPs to a specific target under externally applied magnetic field. Currently, NCT's MNPs are being used for mice studies for imaging of cancerous tumors and their treatment. This theranostics approach is being employed for different cancer therapy, including glioblastoma (brain tumor), The targeted drug delivery can be also used for arthritis, coronary artery diseases, central nervous diseases (e.g., Alzheimer's, Parkinson's), and many ailments.

The high-resolution and high-contrast MRI is being planned to utilize for noninvasive magnetic resonance angiography (MRA) for evaluating blockages in the arteries.

4. How will this revolutionize medicine in 2014 and beyond?

Precise diagnosis and treatment will reduce the cost. The theranostics approach will help the doctors enormously, since they can observe the effect of the drugs on the disease (e.g., cancerous tumor) in real time. The cost of surgical procedures, multiple hospital visits, and use of expensive drug-dosage, etc., will be eliminated or reduced by 10 times or more. There will many more natural plant-based drugs (NPBD), which will create cost-effective medical treatment for the world.

5. How can the greater world benefit from nanotechnology?

Precise treatment at low cost using natural plant-based drugs will change the worldwide health industry. Everyone will be able to afford and procure the same treatment that is available in United States and Europe today.

As mentioned earlier, mobile technology can help us fulfill the dream of affordable health care for all. It's a step in the direction of providing health care services at reasonable cost to everyone, no matter where they live. From my perspective, mobile health care offers many of the same benefits and conveniences as mobile banking. Instead of you going to the doctor's office, the doctor comes to you, via your mobile device. At the risk of sounding too utopian, I believe that truly affordable mobile health care is a vision we can all embrace.

Mobile and Cities of the Future

I don't believe we can have a discussion about our mobile future without including a segment on the future of our cities. And I can think of no one more qualified to discuss the complex relationships between mobile technologies and the evolution of modern cities than Professor Carlo Ratti, director of the SENSE-able City Laboratory at the Massachusetts Institute of Technology. I posed several questions for Carlo recently, and here are his responses:

S.K.: How is mobile technology transforming cities and communities?

C.R.: Back in the 1990s, scholars speculated about the impact of the ongoing digital revolution on the viability of cities. The mainstream view was that, as digital media and the Internet had killed distance, they would also kill cities. Technology writer George Gilder proclaimed that "cities are leftover baggage from the industrial era" and concluded that "we are headed for the death of cities," due to the continued growth of personal computing, telecommunications, and distributed production.

However, cities have never prospered as much as they have over the past couple of decades. China is currently building more urban fabric than has ever been built by humanity. Since 2008, for the first time in history, over half the world's population lives in urban areas. And according to some estimates, there is a US$40 trillion opportunity in global infrastructure investment, mostly urban. The digital revolution did not end up killing our cities, but neither did it leave them unaffected. A layer of networked digital elements has blanketed our environment, blending bits and atoms together in a seamless way. And vast transformations are on the way, which are going to revolutionize urban life—from traffic to the amount of energy we consume to citizen empowerment and participation, as we saw during the Arab Spring. In other words, the city is becoming the place where networks coalesce in space—the catalyst that allows the convergence between the world of bits and that of atoms.

Let me explain this convergence with an analogy. What is happening at an urban scale today is similar to what happened two decades ago in Formula One auto racing. Up to that point, success on the circuit was primarily credited to a car's mechanics and the driver's capabilities. But then telemetry technology blossomed. The car was transformed into a computer that was monitored in real time by thousands of sensors, becoming "intelligent" and better able to respond to the conditions of the race.

In a similar way, over the past decade digital technologies have begun to blanket our cities, forming the backbone of a large, intelligent infrastructure. Broadband fiber-optic and wireless telecommunications grids are supporting mobile phones, smartphones, and tablets that are increasingly affordable. At the same time, open databases—especially from the government—that people can read and add to are revealing all kinds of information, and public kiosks and displays are helping literate and illiterate people access it. Add to this foundation a relentlessly growing network of sensors and digital-control technologies, all tied together by cheap, powerful computers, and our cities are quickly becoming like "computers in open air."

Applications can be manifold: from energy to traffic, from water to waste management. Regarding the latter, at the MIT SENSEable City Lab we mapped the route of the garbage in Seattle, adding tags to trash and then following trash as it moves through the city's sanitation system. One of the things we learned in the trash tracking project is that just sharing information can promote behavioral change. People involved in the project would be able to follow their trash. And this prompted many of them to change their habits. One person told us: "I used to drink water in plastic bottles and throw them away and forget about them. But now I cannot do that anymore: I know that they just go a few miles from home to

133

a landfill. As a result, I have now stopped drinking water in plastic bottles."

The last example highlights that one crucial issue is the approach to smart cities: bottom up or top down?

We believe that people, or citizens, should always be at the center. Rather than focusing on the installation and control of network hardware, city governments, technology companies, and their urban-planning advisers can exploit a more bottom-up approach to creating even smarter cities in which people become the agents of change.

S.K.: What benefits can people expect to see from the application of mobile technologies to urban systems and services?

C.R.: With proper technical-support structures, the population can benefit from having the ability to tackle problems by themselves more effectively than centralized dictates— problems such as energy use, traffic congestion, health care, and education. And residents of wired cities can use their distributed intelligence to fashion new community activities, as well as a new kind of citizen activism.

S.K.: Do you see mobile as a positive force in the evolution of cities?

C.R.: Yes, absolutely. Today's evolution process is very special; in the same way that the car shaped the city of the twentieth century, ICT [information and communications technology] and mobile technologies are reshaping our cities now.

Notes

1. www.fda.gov/downloads/MedicalDevices/DeviceRegulation-andGuidance/GuidanceDocuments/UCM263366.pdf
2. http://steveblank.com/2013/08/20/reinventing-life-science-startups-medical-devices-and-digital-health/

3. http://steveblank.com/2013/12/19/lessons-learned-in-digital-health/
4. A fictional multipurpose device used by the characters on "Star Trek."
5. Neal Kaufman, MD, MPH, "The Diabetes Education and Support Revolution: A New Role for Diabetes Educators," *AADE in Practice*, a publication of the American Association of Diabetes Educators, 2012.

Conclusion

Mobile Is the New Normal

Realizing that my book was nearing its end, I reflected on a conversation I had with my good friend Ganesh Govin, a vice president of digital services and marketing support at Ericsson. I asked Ganesh if he thinks that mobile banking is a fad or part of the new normal. From his perspective, Ganesh believes that mobile has "yes, absolutely" become a permanent feature of the landscape.

"Mobile and digital technologies are expanding into more and more areas of society, business, and private life. This development comes with opportunities for fundamental innovation. New forms of communication will emerge and the arising business opportunities are endless," says Ganesh. "It will change how businesses are organized, as well as how we organize work, collaborate, and share."

Ganesh's colleagues at Ericsson speak of a "networked society" connected by converged technologies and powerful new devices. It's a smarter, more connected, and truly global society with broader opportunities for all.

"In this new society, digital convergence will be the starting point for new ways of innovating, collaborating, and socializing. It is about creating freedom, empowerment, and opportunity, transforming industries and society while helping find solutions to some of the greatest challenges facing our planet," he says.

137

I really love the way Ganesh frames the mobile future in terms of "freedom, empowerment, and opportunity." For me, that vision makes the effort worthwhile. It encourages me to work harder to turn the dream into a reality.

Net Takeaways

What have we learned? Clearly, mobile technology offers us both huge opportunities and significant challenges. Billions of dollars can be earned—or lost. Much will depend on how we approach our mobile strategies.

Looking back over the year I spent researching this book, I realize now that while there is still plenty of room for debate, some points appear inarguable. Among them:

- Mobility is all about convenience. Mobile replaces "going" with "doing." As one writer put it, mobile is about the shift from "places to spaces."
- Mobile banking is about when you want it, where you want it, and how you want it. It is also about when you don't want it, where you don't want it, and how you don't want it.
- Mobile will impact all areas of finance—everything from new virtual currencies to new forms of insurance and new methods of identity management.
- The mobile lifestyle is marked by continuous change, unrelenting transformation, and nonstop improvisation.
- Your mobile identity is fast becoming a combination of your alter ego, your agent, and your personal avatar.
- Your mobile device is becoming a one-stop shopping space for all of your physical and emotional needs.
- Mobile is the new norm. If it can't be done on a mobile device, it probably won't get done at all.
- Government spying on telephone calls is being replaced by government snooping on mobile interactions.

- Terror plots will be formed around destroying mobile databases and creating viruses that adversely affect mobile platforms.
- The biggest fight in the market will be for the best all-encompassing mobile device at the right price point.
- The steady rise in mobile adoption will use up all of the available radio frequency spectrum, requiring the invention and development of a new medium for mobile communications.

Mobile marketing strategy is a topic that I've touched on only lightly, and perhaps it will be the subject of my next book. My friend Ed van Eckert offered some great last-minute advice that I want to include before signing off. Make sure, says Ed, that your mobile banking apps aren't just scaled-down versions of your online banking web pages. Nothing infuriates mobile users more than scaling and rescaling text or buttons on a mobile app that clearly has not been optimized for the device they are using.

Since most people search for apps on Google, Yahoo!, or Bing, make certain that your SEO (search engine optimization) strategy works as well for mobile users as it does for PC users. Finally, make sure that when users find your mobile banking app, they can download it easily and without hassles.

Obviously, some of my observations are optimistic and some are pessimistic. Mobile is a mixed bag, but it's our common future and there's nothing to be gained by avoiding a conversation about the impact of mobility on all of our lives.

In banking, mobile will undoubtedly have a major and long-lasting transformational effect. There will be winners and losers. Fortunes will be gained and lost. We have exciting times ahead of us, and if we're careful and invest wisely, we will enjoy the fruits of a new age of seamless mobility and ubiquitous interactivity. I welcome the future, and look forward to competing successfully in a world connected by increasingly smart networks of increasingly smart mobile devices.

When I began writing this book, only a handful of banks offered customer-friendly mobile services. Today, many more banks have seen the future and are jumping onto the mobile bandwagon, joining thousands of companies that have already blazed the trail and are now reaping the benefits of mobile technologies.

At this very moment, I am sitting in a jetliner, cruising at 400 mph, about 35,000 feet above the southwestern United States. I am checking my e-mail, my Facebook account, my Twitter feed, and stray text messages from family and friends. I am also checking the balance in my bank account. I'm doing all of that on my mobile phone. Something tells me I'm not the only one on the flight who is engaged in some or perhaps all of those same tasks. Together, we are all heading into the mobile future. Enjoy the ride!

Recommended Reading

Carr, Nicholas. *The Big Switch: Rewiring the World, from Edison to Google*. New York, NY: W. W. Norton, 2008.

Christensen, Clayton M. *The Innovator's Dilemma*. New York, NY: Harper Business, 2000.

Christensen, Clayton M., and Michael E. Raynor. *The Innovator's Solution: Creating and Sustaining Successful Growth*. Boston, MA: Harvard Business Review Press, 2003.

Collins, Jim. *Good to Great*. New York, NY: HarperCollins, 2001.

Gregory J. Fell, *Decoding the IT Value Problem: An Executive Guide for Achieving Optimal ROI on Critical IT Investments* (Hoboken, NJ: John Wiley & Sons, 2013).

Gladwell, Malcolm. *Outliers: The Story of Success*. New York, NY: Little, Brown and Company, 2008.

Isaacson, Walter. *Steve Jobs*. New York, NY: Simon & Schuster, 2011.

Kahneman, Daniel. *Thinking, Fast and Slow*. New York, NY: Farrar, Straus and Giroux, 2011.

Moore, Geoffrey A. *Dealing with Darwin: How Great Companies Innovate at Every Phase of Their Evolution*. New York, NY: Portfolio/Penguin, 2005, 2008.

Peppers, Don, and Martha Rogers. *Extreme Trust: Honesty as a Competitive Advantage*. New York, NY: Portfolio/Penguin, 2012.

Prahalad, C. K., and M. S. Krishnan. *The New Age of Innovation: Driving Co-created Value Through Global Networks*. New York: McGraw-Hill, 2008.

Ridley, Matt. *The Rational Optimist: How Prosperity Evolves.* New York: HarperCollins, 2010.

Sharma, Ruchir. *Breakout Nations: In Pursuit of the Next Economic Miracles.* NY: W.W. Norton & Company, 2012, 2013.

Weatherford, Jack. *The History of Money.* NY: Three Rivers Press/Random House, 1997

About the Author

Sankar Krishnan is a career banker and consultant to the banking industry. He is currently Global Head of Engagement/Client Services at HCL America, one of the world's leading technology and business process optimization firms.

He is best known for his work at Citibank, where he served in a variety of executive roles in the Middle East, South Asia, Africa, Europe, and North America. Prior to joining Citibank, he worked at Standard Chartered Bank and Price Waterhouse, now PricewaterhouseCoopers (PwC).

He lives in Scarsdale, New York.

Meet Our Expert Sources

Scott Bales is a self-proclaimed extrovert who has meshed a fascination with people and what motivates them with a raw enthusiasm for technology. He is a founding member of Moven (www.moven.com), the mobile-centric payments business that helps customers to spend, save, and live smarter. He also is a founder at Next Bank (www.nextbank.org), is a mentor to entrepreneurs throughout world with Lean Startup Machine (www.leanstartupmachine.com), sits on the board of education-empowering nongovernmental organization (NGO) Care Pakistan (http://carepakistan.org.uk/), and holds advisory positions at Invitre, Our Better World (http://ourbetterworld.org), HUB Singapore (http://singapore.the-hub.net/), and CDI Apps for Good (http://appsforgood.org/).

Scott's energy transfers to the stage as a globally recognized speaker (www.scottebales.com/speaker) on digital consumers, mobility, and innovation. He has worked with various governments in the Asia-Pacific region and Africa, taking on key advisory roles for countrywide infrastructure and mobile commerce projects. As a multifaceted techie, he was instrumental in developing the mobile commerce space for markets in Malaysia, Singapore, Cambodia, Indonesia, and the Philippines. He is on a mission to transform mainstream thought processing around conventional business practices.

When not in a boardroom or on center stage, you're likely to find Scott devouring, tweeting, and writing (www.scottebales .com) on the latest and greatest in the world of mobility, serendipity, user experience, and entrepreneurial leadership.

Rameshwar N. Bhargava, PhD, founded Nanocrystals Technology
L.P. in 1993. He is the discoverer of doped nanocrystals and quan-
tum confined atoms. Rameshwar served as director and scientific
adviser and also held various scientific and management positions.
Prior to that, he was a member of technical staff at Bell Telephone
Laboratories, IBM Research Center, and IBM Watson Research
Labs. He has been issued 30 U.S. patents and is the author of more
than 100 scientific papers. He is a fellow of the American Physical
Society and the Institute of Electrical and Electronic Engineers.

Steve Blank is a retired eight-time serial entrepreneur-turned-
educator and author; he has changed how start-ups are built
and how entrepreneurship is taught around the globe. Steve
is the author of the best-selling *The Startup Owner's Manual*,
and his earlier seminal work, *The Four Steps to the Epiphany*, is
credited with launching the lean start-up movement. His May
2013 *Harvard Business Review* article "Why the Lean Start-Up
Changes Everything" defined the movement.

Steve is widely recognized as a thought leader on start-ups
and innovation. His books and blog have redefined how to
build successful start-ups; his Lean LaunchPad class at Stanford,
Berkeley, and Columbia has redefined how entrepreneurship is
taught; and his Innovation Corps class for the National Science
Foundation forever changed how the U.S. commercializes
science. His articles regularly appear in the *Wall Street Journal*,
Forbes, *Fortune*, the *Atlantic*, and the *Huffington Post*.

His first book, *The Four Steps to the Epiphany* (2003), offered the
insight that start-ups are not small versions of large companies—
large companies execute business models, but start-ups search
for them—and led him to realize that start-ups need their own
tools, different from those used to manage existing companies.
The book described a customer development methodology to
guide a start-up's search for a scalable business model, launching
the lean start-up movement in the process. His second book,

146

The Startup Owner's Manual (2012), is a step-by-step guide to building a successful company that incorporates the best practices, lessons, and tips that have swept the start-up world since *The Four Steps to the Epiphany* was published. His essays on his blog at www.steveblank.com and his two books are considered required reading among entrepreneurs, investors, and established companies throughout the world.

In 2011, he developed the Lean LaunchPad, a hands-on class that integrates business model design and customer development into practice through rapid, real-world customer interaction and business model iteration. In 2011, the National Science Foundation adopted his class for its Innovation Corps (I-Corps), training teams of the nation's top scientists and engineers to take their ideas out of the university lab and into the commercial marketplace. To date, more than 400 handpicked teams of scientists and engineers have participated in I-Corps.

Steve also offers a free online version of Lean LaunchPad through Udacity.com; more than 100,000 people have signed up for the class, which is also the centerpiece of Startup Weekend NEXT, a global entrepreneurship training program launched in fall 2012.

Steve is a prolific writer, speaker, and teacher. In 2009, he earned the Stanford University Undergraduate Teaching Award in Management Science and Engineering. In 2010, he earned the Earl F. Cheit Outstanding Teaching Award at the University of California at Berkeley Haas School of Business. The *San Jose Mercury News* listed him as one of the 10 Influencers in Silicon Valley. *Harvard Business Review* named him one of 12 Masters of Innovation. Despite these accolades and many others, Steve says he might well have been voted "least likely to succeed" in his New York City high school class.

After repairing fighter plane electronics in Thailand during the Vietnam War, Steve arrived in Silicon Valley in 1978 as boom times began and joined his first of eight start-ups.

147

They included two semiconductor companies, Zilog and MIPS Computers; Convergent Technologies; a consulting stint for Pixar; a supercomputer firm, Ardent; a peripherals supplier, SuperMac; a military intelligence systems supplier, ESL; and Rocket Science Games. Steve cofounded E.piphany, in his living room in 1996. In sum: two significant craters, one massive dot-com bubble home run, several base hits, and immense learning that resulted in *The Four Steps to the Epiphany.*

An avid reader in history, technology, and entrepreneurship, Steve has followed his curiosity about why entrepreneurship blossomed in Silicon Valley while it was stillborn elsewhere. It has made him an unofficial expert and frequent speaker on "The Secret History of Silicon Valley."

Steve served as a commissioner of the California Coastal Commission, the public body that regulates land use and public access on the California coast. He is on the board of the California League of Conservation Voters (CLCV), is a past board member of Audubon California and the Peninsula Open Space Trust (POST), and was a trustee of the University of California at Santa Cruz.

Steve's proudest start-ups are daughters Katie and Sarah, codeveloped with wife Alison Elliott. They split their time between Pescadero and Silicon Valley.

Annetta Cortez is the founder and managing director of ACT Consulting, and author of both *Winning at Risk: Strategies to Go Beyond Basel* and *The Complete Idiot's Guide to Risk Management.*

An experienced professional in the area of risk and capital management, Annetta works closely with major financial institutions and regulatory authorities around the world. As such, she has worked with her clients on a wide range of risk management issues, including operational risk, Internet banking, and mobile applications, among other risk management disciplines.

She holds an MBA in finance, strategic management, and international management from the Wharton School of Business as well as a bachelor of science degree in chemical engineering from the University of Rochester.

Michael Faye is the cofounder and chairman of GiveDirectly, which has recently been recognized as a top nonprofit by GiveWell, the fourth most innovative company in finance (after Bitcoin and Square), and awarded a Google Global Impact Award. He was recently announced as a top 100 Global Thinker by *Foreign Policy*. Michael is an associate partner at McKinsey and Company and holds a PhD in business economics from Harvard University. His work focused on international development and aid and has been published by the *American Economic Review* and *Brookings Papers*.

Greg Fell is the Chief Strategy Officer at Crisply, an enterprise software-as-a-service (SaaS) big data company that pioneered the algorithmic quantification of work. Prior to joining Crisply in 2013, Greg served as Vice President and Chief Information Officer of Terex Corporation, where he led a strategic transformation of the IT organization. Terex is a manufacturer of industrial equipment that employs 23,000 persons in 50 manufacturing locations around the globe.

Before joining Terex, Greg spent nearly 20 years with Ford Motor Company. He started as a developer, and worked his way through a variety of management roles supporting the global engineering and manufacturing functions of the company. He has domain expertise on CAD/CAM/CAE systems, lean manufacturing, and control systems.

He is a graduate of Michigan State University, and spent several years on staff in the College of Engineering as a senior research programmer and instructor.

Greg is active in the CIO community, and is frequently quoted in books and periodicals for his knowledge of implementing ERP projects and general IT leadership strategies. He is a recent president of the Fairfield Westchester Society of Information Managers, a board member with Junior Achievement, and a mentor of high school students through the First Tee Program.

He is the author of *Decoding the IT Value Problem: An Executive Guide for Achieving Optimal ROI on Critical IT Investments* (John Wiley & Sons, 2013).

Ganesh Govin is Vice President of Digital Services and Marketing Support, Global Customer Unit Etisalat (Emirates Telecommunications Corporation) at Ericsson. He is responsible for building a trusted partner relationship with Etisalat Digital services and Group Marketing to establish Ericsson as a credible brand and to secure profitable business for Ericsson. One of his primary duties is assisting customers to realize Ericsson's Networked Society Vision, addressing both the key stakeholders' interest and benefiting society at large. His areas of expertise include business development, sales and marketing, brand management, strategic account development, relationship selling, upselling and consultative selling, mobile Internet consulting, and customer solution sales.

Ganesh holds a bachelor's degree in engineering from Bharathidasan University and an MBA in marketing from Madurai Kamaraj University.

Matthew Holt is the creator of the Healthcare Blog, as well as a health care researcher, forecaster, and strategist. He conducts in-depth studies regarding many aspects in health care for both public release and private clients, and he publishes his analysis and opinions daily on his blog. He began his health care career conducting international health policy research at Stanford University's Shorenstein Asia-Pacific Research Center.

At the Institute for the Future think tank, he led projects in health care financing, delivery, and information technology. He also conducted two landmark survey research studies at Harris Interactive, Computing in the Physician's Practice, and The 10,000 Patients Study. He was also vice president for strategy and business development at i-Beacon.com before returning to consulting.

Farhad Irani is the Executive Vice President and Group Head of Retail Banking at Mashreq Bank—the United Arab Emirates' largest and fastest-growing privately owned financial institution, with operations in 12 countries and adjudged the Best Regional Retail Bank by the *Banker Middle East* in 2012 and the Most Innovative Retail Bank in the Region in 2013.

He has over 29 years' work experience in the payments, retail banking, and e-commerce space, having delivered through executive positions at Mashreq Bank (EVP and Group Head, Retail Bank), PayPal (a division of eBay Inc. as Asia General Manager), Standard Chartered Bank (Global Head, Credit Cards and Personal Loans, and Group Head, Consumer Finance), Citibank Japan (Chief Marketing Officer), and Korea Exchange Bank (Chief Marketing Officer).

He has lived and worked in India, Indonesia, South Korea, Japan, Singapore, Hong Kong, Dubai, and Australia. He is enthusiastic about starting up and turning around companies in distress or in start-up mode, garnering highly effective management teams, defining strategic deliverables, and executing passionately.

Adjudged a Marketing Superstar by *Advertising Age* in 1995, he has a master's degree in management studies (Mumbai University, majoring in finance and marketing), a bachelor's degree in science, executive management degrees in management from the London Business School and from INSEAD (France), AIB, and CAIIB. He is based in Dubai at present. Farhad loves travel, golf, and engaging with new cultures.

Neal Kaufman, MD, MPH, founder and Chief Medical Officer of DPS Health, is an experienced clinician, educator, and leader in local, state, and national efforts to improve the health of vulnerable individuals and communities. He is an innovator in web and cell phone solutions that enable clinicians to help patients adopt and sustain health-promoting behaviors and to improve long-term health outcomes. Additionally, he is an expert in a range of areas including educating patients and health care providers, improving the provision of health and social services and creating innovative solutions to complex problems. In 2004, after his 27-year career in academic primary care, he founded DPS Health to help at-risk individuals by creating health communications technology solutions to prevent and treat chronic disease. He is cofounder of the UCLA Center for Healthier Children, Families and Communities, and is a professor of pediatrics and public health at the UCLA Schools of Medicine and Public Health.

Brett King is a global best-selling author, a well-known futurist and speaker, the host of the *Breaking Bank$* radio show on VoiceAmerica (an Internet talk radio network with over nine million monthly listeners), and the founder of the start-up Moven. Brett was voted *American Banker*'s Innovator of the Year in 2012, and was nominated by Bank Innovation as one of the top 10 "coolest brands in banking." Since its release late in 2012 from John Wiley & Sons, *Bank 3.0* (in eight languages) has been topping the charts in the United States, United Kingdom, China, Canada, Germany, Japan, and France. His latest book, *Breaking Banks*, is due out in early 2014 from John Wiley & Sons. He is widely considered the world's foremost expert on retail banking innovation today.

Harvey Koeppel is the President of Pictographics, Inc., a management and technology advisory and consulting services firm. The firm has provided executive-level support to the financial services industry since its inception in 1979. Harvey is a frequent speaker at leading U.S. and global industry forums and a frequent contributor to major IT industry and general news publications.

He has served on numerous advisory boards for Fortune 500 companies, including IBM, Unisys, AT&T, Oracle, and many others. He has served on the Advisory Council of the New York State Office of Technology/Office of the CIO, and has been a featured guest lecturer at prominent colleges and universities globally, including Harvard Business School, Carnegie Mellon University, Stanford University, Pepperdine, Cranfield University, and INSEAD.

Harvey currently provides executive advisory and management consulting services to audit, risk, and executive committees of major financial services firms. In that capacity he performs regular independent reviews of current IT and operations capabilities and future plans, and advises directors on areas of specific opportunities and challenges.

From October 2007 through June 2012, Harvey cofounded with IBM and served as Executive Director of the Center for CIO Leadership. He set the Center's strategy and directed internal and external operations in support of a global community serving more than 3,000 CIOs and other C-level executives. The community served an engaged membership representing more than 75 countries across 50 industries across private and public sectors.

From May 2004 through June 2007, he served as the Chief Information Officer and Senior Vice President of Citigroup's Global Consumer Group (GCG). In that role, he set the strategic direction for the GCG's operations and technology and actively supported the development and growth of the operations and technology community across all GCG lines of business in 54 countries serving 180 million customers. He had oversight of a $2.8 billion budget.

Harvey has a distinguished record of IT innovation in the financial services industry. He designed the first graphical user interface for the NASDAQ trader workstation. He was the architect and designer of FxNet, a software program that revolutionized the way large financial institutions manage settlement risk within foreign exchange (FX) portfolios. Harvey is the named inventor on the Citibank patent of the Recommendation Engine, a software component that advises sales and service staff about products and services to discuss with clients based on their financial goals and objectives.

Harvey holds bachelor's degrees in psychology and computer science from the University of Pittsburgh.

Art Mannarn is Chief Administrative Officer and Executive Vice President, Retail and Business Banking at Canadian Imperial Bank of Commerce (CIBC). In this role, Art leads the development and execution of key strategic initiatives and high-impact projects to optimize resources and operational efficiency. He is accountable for ensuring that the Retail and Business Banking function has an infrastructure with appropriate technology platforms, processes, controls, and measures to enable frontline delivery of a consistently positive client experience across all channels.

In addition, Art leads the Business Support and Strategic Initiatives team, which includes Retail and Business Banking's project and program management offices and is focused on client experience, operational capability, process improvement, frontline channel support, and client account management.

Since joining CIBC in 1989, he has held progressively more senior executive roles in both operations and sales. Prior to his current role, he was Executive Vice President, CIBC Global Operations and INTRIA, and Senior Vice President, CIBC Corporate Services. He has also held the positions of Deputy Head of CIBC Wood Gundy, Managing Director of CIBC World Markets, and President and Chief Operating Officer of CIBC Investor Services Inc.

Art has more than 25 years of experience in the financial services industry, which he pursued after graduating from the University of Toronto. He is past president of Ronald McDonald House Toronto, has led a team of 26 climbers up the slopes of Mount Kilimanjaro on the inaugural CIBC Wood Gundy Climb

154

for the Cure, and has been instrumental in the launch of the Minor Hockey Fights Cancer charitable initiative. Art is actively involved in minor hockey in Toronto.

Jim Marous is an internationally recognized financial industry strategist and SVP of corporate development for the direct and digital marketing agency New Control. He specializes in developing innovative, multichannel solutions that drive revenue through acquisition, engagement, and expanding share of wallet and retention for the financial services industry. He has helped to successfully launch new products and services as well as built and reinforced existing products and brands.

His specialties include new customer acquisition, relationship activation, customer lifecycle marketing (CRM), multichannel integration, new brand or product launch, win-back and retention strategies, and new business development. Beyond financial services, his industry experience includes retail, hospitality, and B2B marketing in the United States and Canada.

As a frequent industry speaker, author of the award-winning *Bank Marketing Strategy* blog and recognized authority on measured media, Jim works with clients and key marketing executives in trying to use customer and prospect insight to drive bottom line results. He can also be followed on Twitter and LinkedIn.

Phillip M. Miller is Global Head of the Acquiring Knowledge Center at MasterCard Advisors. MasterCard's Knowledge Centers distill the experience and insights from decades of real-world engagements into global best practices. In his current role, Phillip focuses on consulting merchant acquirers globally and is responsible for thought leadership for strategic business development and emerging technologies.

In his prior role as Group Head of U.S. Commerce Development for MasterCard, he was responsible for the disciplines of e-commerce, business development, and marketing across a broad spectrum of key retail and e-commerce customers. In

2005, he joined MasterCard Advisors as global solutions leader. In this role, he headed the consulting practice that provided information services for large bank acquirers globally.

He has executive management experience in both business-to-business and consumer financial services. His skills are in the area of profit-and-loss (P&L) management in the card acquiring business, credit cards, private label cards, consumer lending, private banking, and branch distribution in the United States and internationally. Phillip also has mergers and acquisitions experience in due diligence, valuation, acquisition, and integration of financial institutions internationally. He has launched credit cards, debit cards, prepaid cards, lending, and mutual fund products in both the physical world and online globally.

Prior to joining MasterCard, Phillip held the position of President and CEO of Chase Merchant services, a division of JPMorgan Chase, the largest bank acquiring business in the United States; Senior Vice President, Global Marketing for GE Money, GE Capital's Global Consumer Financial Services Group; and Vice President of International Product Development for Citibank's International Private Bank.

He graduated from American University in Washington, D.C., with an MBA in international business and finance. He earned his undergraduate degree from American University in marketing and management.

Stan Nowak is Chief Executive Officer and Cofounder of Silverlink Communications. His vision is to help health plans, pharmacy companies, and other key health care stakeholders become trusted health advisers as they improve health, reduce health care costs, and build loyalty with their members. His innovation is to bring the power of consumer marketing methodologies to health care communications. This vision has helped 21 of the top 25 health plans better engage their members and drive improved outcomes.

156

Under Stan's leadership, Silverlink has developed a flexible communications technology, proprietary analytics capabilities, and a team with deep industry expertise.

Stan's background includes over 22 years of general and executive management in technology services. He held executive roles with StorageNetworks, GTE, and InterGen (Bechtel). He is often quoted by the health care and business press, and is a frequent keynote speaker at industry events. Stan holds a master's degree from Harvard Business School and a bachelor's degree from Harvard College.

Stan's year of studying at Harvard while caring for and living with his ailing grandfather had a profound effect in his decision, years later, to found Silverlink Communications with business colleague Paulo Matos. Today Silverlink is the proven leader in engagement management solutions for health care organizations. Its solutions enable health plans and other key stakeholders to engage and support their members in smarter and more effective ways. The stakes have never been higher to ensure that health plans deliver better control, coordination, and effectiveness in member communications to promote healthy and loyal behaviors. More than 100 health care clients, including the top 10 U.S. health plans, count on Silverlink to help them better engage with their members. All told, Silverlink has influenced more than 600 million health care decisions across the country.

Todd Nuttall brings more than 20 years of experience in domestic and international finance, payments systems, technology innovation, and leadership to his position as president and chief executive officer of Better ATM Services.

Formerly vice president of financial and strategic services for American Express, Mr. Nuttall led efforts to transform payment processing, financial reconciliation, and reporting in India, the UK, and North America. He also served as vice president and CFO of American Express Worldwide Data Operations, which included oversight on technology spending approaching $1 billion annually. Mr. Nuttall's previously held technology leadership roles include Boeing Computer Systems, Ernst & Young LLP, and Phelps Dodge Corporation.

Don Peppers is a best-selling business author and founding partner of Peppers & Rogers Group, the world's foremost customer-centered management consulting firm. Don is recognized as a global authority on marketing and business competition, and widely credited with having launched the customer relationship management (CRM) revolution in the 1990s. A genuine thought leader, he was listed by *The Times of London* as one of the Top 50 Business Brains. Accenture named him one of the Top 100 Business Intellectuals, and the United Kingdom's Chartered Institute for Marketing called him one of the 50 "most influential thinkers in marketing and business today."

Don is a popular voice in the worldwide media, writing articles, sharing his point of view, and appearing frequently as an "expert blogger" for Fastcompany.com. He is the author or coauthor of a legacy of international business best sellers that have collectively sold over a million copies in 18 languages: *Extreme Trust: Honesty as a Competitive Advantage* (2012), *Managing Customer Relationships* (2011), *Rules to Break & Laws to Follow* (2008), *Return on Customer* (2005), *One to One B2B* (2001), *The One to One Manager* (1999), *The One to One Fieldbook* (1999), *Enterprise One to One* (1997), *Life's a Pitch: Then You Buy* (1995), and *The One to One Future* (1993).

Banesh Prabhu is senior executive vice president—group head technology & operations at Siam Commercial Bank PCL in Thailand. Banesh is a member of the Executive Committee of Siam Commercial Bank and is responsible for the bank's Technology and Operations Group, since June 2013. He is a technology management and financial solutions veteran with over 30 years' experience globally. Siam Commercial Bank is the leading Universal banking group in Thailand, with the largest branch and ATM network along with a full range of banking products and businesses along with insurance, brokerage, and securities subsidiary businesses.

Banesh has held several senior global roles in Operations & Technology in Citibank for 23 years, where he was responsible to develop and implement a global strategy for servicing clients in international markets. During these years he pioneered and led the creation of several global hubs for operations, technology, and shared services across the world.

In his last role with Citibank he was the international operations head for the consumer business and developed and implemented the global operations and servicing strategy for over 50 countries across all regions ex-North America. The international consumer business serviced over 80 million customers through 35,000 employees. Prior to this, he was the global operations director for international cards and before that the operations and technology director for Central and Eastern Europe, Middle East, Africa, and the Indian subcontinent. Prior to that he was the operations and systems director in India, during which he created several tech companies and a BPO for the bank.

He has also been a keen entrepreneur and investor in many start-ups.

Banesh is a chartered accountant, a bachelor of general law, and a bachelor of commerce and prior to Citibank worked for several years with American Express and a leading international audit and consulting company.

Narayanan Ram is CEO and a Founder of PurpleTeal, a U.S.-based health messaging services provider. He was previously the Founder, Chairman, and CEO of SeeItFirst Inc., a video software tools company. He founded SeeItFirst in 1997, raised millions of dollars in capital, launched the first product in 1998, and put together a strong management team and board of directors. SeeItFirst was acquired by UB Group in 2001. He continued as CEO of SeeItFirst until 2004. Before founding SeeItFirst, he had worked for Cirrus Logic at various positions from 1993 to 1996, and helped deliver the first videoconferencing chip for Cirrus Logic.

He has an MS in electrical engineering and holds several patents (issued and pending).

Carlo Ratti is an architect and engineer by training. He practices in Italy and teaches at the Massachusetts Institute of Technology, where he directs the SENSEable City Lab. He graduated with a degree in engineering from the Politecnico di Torino and the École Nationale des Ponts et Chaussées in Paris, and later earned his MPhil and PhD in architecture at the University of Cambridge, United Kingdom. Carlo holds several patents and has coauthored over 250 publications. As well as being a regular contributor to the architecture magazine *Domus* and the Italian newspaper *Il Sole 24 Ore*, he has written for the BBC, *La Stampa*, *Scientific American*, and the *New York Times*. His work has been exhibited worldwide at venues such as the Venice Biennale, the Design Museum in Barcelona, the Science Museum in London, Gray Area Foundation for the Arts (GAFTA) in San Francisco, and the Museum of Modern Art in New York. Carlo has been featured in *Esquire* magazine's 2008 Best & Brightest list and in Thames & Hudson's selection of "60 innovators" shaping our creative future.

In 2010, *Blueprint* magazine included him as one of the 25 People Who Will Change the World of Design, *Forbes* listed him as one of the Names You Need to Know in 2011, and *Fast Company* named him as one of the 50 Most Influential Designers in America. He was also featured in *Wired* magazine's "Smart List 2012: 50 people who will change the world." His Digital Water Pavilion at the 2008 World Expo was hailed by *Time* magazine as one of the Best Inventions of the Year.

In 2011, Carlo was awarded the Renzo Piano Foundation prize for New Talents in Architecture. Carlo has been a presenter at

TED (2011), program director at the Strelka Institute for Media, Architecture and Design in Moscow, and curator of the 2012 BMW Guggenheim Pavilion in Berlin, and he was named Inaugural Innovator in Residence by the Queensland Government. The Italian Minister of Culture also named Carlo as a member of the Italian Design Council, an advisory board to the Italian Government that includes 25 leaders of design in Italy. He is currently serving as a member of the World Economic Forum Global Agenda Council for Urban Management and is a curator for the Future Food District pavilion for the 2015 World Expo in Milan. For further information on Carlo's projects, visit www.carloratti.com and senseable.mit.edu.

Kurt R. Schneiber is top-performing international business leader and growth strategist dedicated to creating profitable organizations across cultures since 1985, recruited to jump-start organizations in North America, Europe, Africa, Asia, and the Middle East. He has a long track record of success in the financial, technology, and packaged goods industries, and served as chairman of the board for international financial organizations with multibillion-dollar volume businesses.

As chair of the board of ELM Resources, he built consensus among a broad group of competitors/owners to accomplish common objectives, and guided restructuring of the company's technology investments.

Kurt was named among the top 100 most influential people in finance by *Treasury & Risk* magazine (2011) and led negotiations with some of the world's largest banks to establish the first multibank network for global supply chain finance.

Kurt is responsible for guiding the cultural transformation of financial service and technology organizations to a culture of innovation and empowerment, resulting in a turnaround from negative to positive performance and positioning the companies for sustainable growth. His career has included senior-level executive positions at Syncada, a joint venture of U.S. Bank and

Visa; Fortent, a privately held technology firm; Citigroup, Inc.; and Gerber Products Company.

Mick Simonelli is a global thought leader on innovation in large organizations who works as an independent consultant for Fortune 500 companies. For the past five years, Mick served as the senior innovation executive for USAA, where he built and led the innovation program to world-class status. Before that, Mick served as a lead innovator in multiple positions within the Department of Defense, where he helped digitize and transform the U.S. Army.

Mick is a certified management accountant and possesses advanced degrees in business and psychology. A natural change agent, Mick is an executive innovation practitioner with his innovation programs receiving numerous awards and accolades. Mick's work has appeared on NPR, *American Banker, Workforce Magazine, Fast Company, Information Week 500*, and has been the subject of numerous academic articles.

Chris Skinner is best known as an independent commentator on the financial markets through the Finanser (www.thefinanser .com) and as Chair of the European networking forum the Financial Services Club, which he founded in 2004. The Financial Services Club, a network for financial professionals, focuses on the future of financial services through the delivery of research, analysis, commentary, and debate, and has regular meetings in London, Edinburgh, Dublin, and Vienna. He is the author of 10 books on subjects ranging from European regulations in banking through the credit crisis to the future of banking. He is also Chief Executive of Balatro Ltd, a research company, and a cofounder of the website Shaping Tomorrow, as well as a regular commentator on BBC News, Sky News, and Bloomberg about banking issues.

He is a judge on many awards programs, including the Card Awards and the Asian Banker's Retail Excellence Awards, as well as having worked closely with leading banks such as HSBC, the

Royal Bank of Scotland, Citibank, and Société Générale, and with the World Economic Forum.

Chris is known for regular speaking and keynote presentations at leading industry forums. Through these keynotes, he has presented alongside many other leading world figures, including Gary Hamel, Michael Porter, Richard Branson, Lou Gerstner, Meg Whitman, and Bill Gates. He is a judge with many industry awards programs, as well as a contributor to the World Economic Forum.

Prior to founding Balatro, Chris was Vice President of Marketing and Strategy for Unisys Global Financial Services and Strategy Director with NCR Financial Services. These roles sparked Chris's specialization in the future of financial services after he created the Global Future Forum in Unisys and the Knowledge Lab in NCR.

He studied at Loughborough University in the United Kingdom, and holds a bachelor of science in management sciences alongside a diploma in industrial studies. He is a Fellow of the British Computer Society, a Fellow of the Institute of Management Services, an Associate of the Chartered Insurance Institute, and a Chartered Insurance Practitioner. More can be discovered about Chris Skinner at http://thefinanser.co.uk/fsclub/chris-skinner/.

Steven J. Smith is a seasoned bank card executive with international experience and an industry leader in the development and implementation of new business initiatives.

As principal of S.J. Smith & Associates, Steve works with leading card issuers worldwide developing and implementing practical solutions that achieve measurable results in a variety of areas, including credit and debit card business strategy, co-branding, product development, customer and financial management, customer service, and sales training.

Steve regularly conducts business process reviews that are designed to benchmark and assess the full range of card management functions and to install leading-edge skills and processes that enhance business results.

He leads innovative seminars worldwide on segmentation, cobranding, generating fee income, and best practices associated with managing the card life cycle of acquisition, activation, usage, and retention. He is the author and host of several training videos, and his most recent publication, *Marketing Cobranded and Affinity Cards in the US*.

Steve has directed the American Banker's Association Bankcard School at Emory University and taught segmentation and credit and debit card profitability at the Visa Europe Business School at Cambridge University.

Steve earned both an Echo and a Clio award for his work in direct marketing. S.J. Smith & Associates' clients include leading issuers in Europe, Asia, the United States, and Latin America.

Working with locally owned banks or with the local operations of international banks, S.J. Smith & Associates has conducted marketing and risk assignments and organizational reviews, developed and installed scoring and segmentation schemes, and brokered or advised on cobranded card programs in a wide range of markets.

Steve founded S.J. Smith & Associates in 1992 following a career at Citibank, where he held a variety of management positions and was responsible for introducing cobranding with the American Airlines AAdvantage Card. He was the founding Business Manager of Citibank's bank card business in Spain and was responsible for all aspects of the business in addition to serving as a senior corporate officer responsible for country policy and as a Visa España board member.

Danny Tang is a renowned thought leader in banking transformation. He currently leads the channel transformation and front office digitization solutions for IBM's Global Banking organization. In this role, he advises banks around the world on pressing issues such as mobile, social business, branch banking, and other insight-driven transformation in the front office.

Prior to his current role, Danny was assigned to China as the executive leading IBM Software Group's Financial Services Industry Solutions team as well as the leader of China Bank Modernization Program.

He is the author of two patents, speaks at many conferences, and events and has authored numerous business and technical articles. As a member of the prestigious IBM IT Architect Board, he also participates in setting strategic directions for the IT Architect profession within IBM.

Danny holds an MBA with concentration in finance and operations management from the Anderson School at UCLA. He lives in the San Francisco Bay Area.

His recent publications include Banking Gets Social (BXW12346USEN), Banking on the Customer (GBW03183USEN), Revolution of the Customer Focused Enterprise (BXW12345USEN), The Challenge for a Competitive Edge in Transaction Banking (BKW03021USEN), Mobile Money (GBW03221USEN), and blogs on ibm.com (insights-on-business.com/banking/author/dtang/).

Jonathan Teich, MD, PhD, is Chief Medical Information Officer of Elsevier and a physician at Brigham and Women's Hospital in Boston, Massachusetts. His areas of expertise include health information infrastructure, e-prescribing, and clinical decision support systems.

Jonathan's primary focus lies in the design of innovative information systems to directly improve clinical care, prevent adverse events, and streamline clinical work flow to address the most critical needs of the health care community.

He is the author or co-author of more than 100 peer-reviewed papers, books, and editorials in the field of medical informatics and health care information systems.

Jonathan serves on a number of industry and government leadership councils. He is cochair of the panel responsible for the U.S. Department of Health and Human Services–sponsored Roadmap for National Action on Clinical Decision Support, a board member of the eHealth Initiative, a fellow of the American College of Medical Informatics and of HIMSS, and a member of the American Health Information Community Quality Workgroup.

Jim Tosone is Managing Director at Tosone Associates. He is the creator of the Improv Means Business program, which helps organizations enhance their innovation, collaboration, and communication capabilities using the principles and techniques of applied improvisation. His clients include major corporations such as Dannon, DirecTV, MetLife, M&M Mars, PepsiCo, Pfizer, and Time Warner.

He was a Pfizer Business Technology executive for 30 years; his last position was head of Pfizer Healthcare Informatics. He is a graduate of The Second City Training Center, the world's leading improvisation organization. Jim holds BS and MS degrees from Stevens Institute of Technology in Hoboken, New Jersey.

Edward van Eckert is a global marketing consultant specializing in social media and thought leadership implementation. He has provided marketing expertise to PricewaterhouseCoopers, Mellon Bank, Deloitte, Mercer, Novantas, Farmers Insurance, and Pitney Bowes Financial Services among others. He is a graduate of St. John's University in New York City and has studied social media marketing at Rutgers University Center for Management Development.

Index